Presented to:

_____

From:

_____

Date:

_____

Finding Calm in a Busy Day

DAILY REFLECTIONS *on*
REST, HOPE, AND LOVE

Abingdon Press
Growing in Life, Serving in Faith

NASHVILLE

Library of Congress Cataloging-in-Publication Data has been requested

ISBN 978-1-5018-9417-6

19 20 21 22 23 24 25 26 —10 9 8 7 6 5 4 3 2 1

MANUFACTURED IN THE PEOPLE'S REPUBLIC OF CHINA

Finding Calm in a Busy Day

DAILY REFLECTIONS *on* REST, HOPE, AND LOVE

Take a Break with Jesus

*Many people were coming and going, so there was
no time to eat. He said to the apostles, "Come by yourselves
to a secluded place and rest for a while."*

—Mark 6:31

Do you ever get so caught up in your hectic day that you don't have time to eat? There's a deadline for a big project that gives you little time to think about anything else. Or a child forgets her lunch or homework assignment, and now you're dashing off to school. Maybe you even forget what day it is. You have to remind yourself who needs to be where for what activity.

No matter how busy you get, no matter how crazy the day becomes, you need to take a moment or two to spend with Jesus. He knows you need to spend time with him to find encouragement, refreshment, and direction—just as the disciples needed to go off with Jesus to rest awhile. The more chaotic the day, the more the waves of concern crash against you, the more you need to ask him to quiet the waters.

Let's be mindful of what God has done even in the middle of the busiest of times. Take time to be alone with the Lord. That may mean no more than closing your eyes and momentarily

Get away with Jesus and rest awhile.

shutting out the distractions all around you. Tell him thank you. Celebrate the fact that we are surrounded by the abundance he provided. Rest in his promise to be with you always, no matter what you're going through.

QUIET THE WAVES

Lord, I get caught up in the to-do list of my daily life, and I forget to spend time with you and simply rest in your presence. I thank you for all you do to make it possible for me to live more fully and richly. Bless this day and walk with me. Amen.

Saved in Hope

We know that the whole creation is groaning together and suffering labor pains up until now. And it's not only the creation. We ourselves who have the Spirit as the first crop of the harvest also groan inside as we wait to be adopted and for our bodies to be set free. We were saved in hope.

—Romans 8:22-24

Whether we are conscious of it or not, we all have hope. We hope that the work we do will make a difference or that it will at least be accomplished well. We hope that our children will be strong and healthy and grow up to be kind and generous people. We hope that we'll get to enjoy more of life as the days ahead unfold because we've been mired in things that don't make life easy. Whatever it is and wherever we are, we live in hope.

In Paul's letter to the Romans, though, he takes that idea a step further. He says we were saved in hope. We were saved in hope and we long for our spirits to be set free. We anticipate the coming of Christ as the moment when we can be all that we were meant to be in his eyes. We hope that we are blessed in the harvest and picked to be with our Lord forever. We live in hope.

You have the hope of eternal life as a child of God.

We are anchored in the hope of our Redeemer. Let us live and work and play in that hope every day.

QUIET THE WAVES

Lord, I am so grateful for the hope I have in you. I know that if all else fails, if I cannot accomplish all that I hope to achieve, still I am eternally safe in your care. I have put all my hope in your hands. Amen.

The Race of God's Grace

I also observed under the sun that the race doesn't always
go to the swift, nor the battle to the mighty, nor food to the wise,
nor wealth to the intelligent, nor favor to the knowledgeable.

—Ecclesiastes 9:11

The writer of Ecclesiastes reminds us that the sun shines on everybody, and it doesn't necessarily just shine on the people who deserve it. When we prepare for a race, a new job, or an opportunity that puts us out in front of others, we may forget one thing. We may forget how much our ego is also invested in the outcome. We may even start to become people who believe life owes us and that we're entitled to the good stuff.

What we're entitled to is God's grace, given freely, no matter who we are. Others may get ahead of us, but it could be by accident as the passage suggests, or it could be by design. After all, the Creator of the universe has every tool at his disposal for good or ill. He can bring out the rain and the sun whenever he chooses.

Today, as you examine your effort at the things you do, don't worry about who else might win at the game you are playing. Just trust and believe that it's important for you to be the best you can possibly be. Your Heavenly Father knows why.

Let go of your worries because you have received God's grace.

QUIET THE WAVES

Lord, help me stop comparing myself to others and be willing to bring only my best to you no matter what. Amen.

When You Don't Know How to Pray

We don't know what we should pray, but the Spirit itself
pleads our case with unexpressed groans.

—Romans 8:26

Our instincts are heightened, our thoughts are somewhat vaguely tuned in to someone we love or something that we just can't put our fingers on, and yet we have a feeling we should stop everything and pray. But for what, or for whom?

When the Holy Spirit nudges you to pray with some insistence, it's good to listen. You may come to the Lord with a vague awareness that you were meant to pray only to discover that you still don't know exactly what brought you to your knees. All you know now is that you haven't hit on whatever it was and so you wait, hoping it will come to you.

The good news is that your obedience is all that was needed. The Spirit has directed it so that your heart and God's will are aligned. You have served as a prayer warrior for someone out in the world.

John Calvin wrote, "God tolerates even our stammering, and pardons our ignorance whenever something inadvertently escapes us." We are blessed with a freedom to address our God at any time. We can put all things in front of him because he cares so much about us. Prayer is one of your best habits.

Always be ready to pray when the Spirit urges you.

QUIET THE WAVES

Lord, I thank you for hearing me and accepting my most humble prayers. Thanks for all your blessings to me. Amen.

Another To-Do List

People plan their path, but the Lord secures their steps.

—Proverbs 16:9

Are you a list maker? You know, you write out the things you'll do tomorrow, jotting notes to yourself about what you hope to achieve. You may not get all of it done, but at least it's on a list. Then you walk out the door, and you forget to take the list. You strive to remember each thing you had so carefully noted, but somehow still arrive back home with the most important one of all left undone.

Setting goals and making plans are both good things. In fact, it's wise indeed to make plans for the things you anticipate. The proverb here, though, reminds us of one important fact. Planning provides an invitation to pray. Only God can secure the way for you and create the opportunities that will bring the desired result.

What if you start your to-do list like this: Things I have to do tomorrow. No. 1: Pray. No. 2: Thank God for today, because he

created it for me. No. 3: Get some guidance about the things on my
to-do list.

It's a new day and a new opportunity to make some plans. Include your
heavenly Father in your to-do list and it
won't matter if you leave the house without your list. He knows what you need
to get done.

*P*ut prayer at the top
of your to-do list.

QUIET THE WAVES

*Lord, you know that I have a lot of things to accomplish today. I know
that I can't do one of them without you. Please be with me today and
help me get all my tasks done. Amen.*

Clinging to the Vine

Now choose life—so that you and your descendants
will live—by loving the Lord your God, by obeying
his voice, and by clinging to him.

—Deuteronomy 30:19-20

Life is full of amusement to those who observe it philosophically. It is a reason to laugh out loud. For those who filter everything through the lens of the heart, through the things that touch every nerve in their being, it can be overwhelming, even tragic. Life is not easy for the sensitive of heart. Yet, for those who seek God first, who cling to the Vinedresser and press forward, it is indeed a victory.

The Vinedresser presents you with daily choices, designed to help you experience more of what he has for you. He offers you an abundant journey as you listen to him and to voices that resonate with you and stay steadily on the path. Every day, perhaps even every hour, you are asked to choose. What will you cling to?

Believers in Christ may differ in the practice or the intensity of their system of belief, but they all have one thing in common. As believers, they all have the victory through Jesus. This is your day to proclaim the victory and to let others know your choice to do so.

Choose to follow Jesus as you go through the day.

Live today in the joy of the Lord.

QUIET THE WAVES

Lord, you have opened your arms to me, ready to guide me to the victory that comes from knowing you. Help me keep making the choices that will bring me safely home. Amen.

Seek First to Understand

Fools find no pleasure in understanding,
but only in expressing their opinion.

—Proverbs 18:2

Some people never tire of sharing their opinion on the topic of the day, whether anyone asked them for it or not.

Wisdom doesn't care so much about opinions. Wisdom always seeks first to understand. Understanding something is a layered process. You can understand the first layer, but once you've peeled it off, somewhat like an onion skin, and gone to the next layer, you may have to start again to grasp the deeper concept. God designed us to strive to understand one another. He wanted us to dig in and work for a clearer meaning to things.

Intellect may help, but intelligence doesn't necessarily bring true understanding to the table. We must seek understanding like thirsty explorers, hoping to come upon nuggets of truth that we simply couldn't see before even if they were right in front of us.

For a person of faith, understanding is a treasure to be sought after, precious in all that it brings.

Keep your heart and mind in Christ Jesus for greater understanding.

QUIET THE WAVES

Lord, I do seek to understand more of you today and to be more closely attuned to others as I go about my work. I ask you to help me offer an attitude of understanding more than an ungrounded opinion. Amen.

The Feast of Happiness

An understanding heart seeks knowledge;
but fools feed on folly. All the days of the needy are hard,
but a happy heart has a continual feast.

—Proverbs 15:14-15

When we choose to feast on happiness more than folly, we are blessed with abundance and always satisfied. We have a banquet of opportunities to fill us with delight. We smell the savory goodness of all that is before us, appreciating the beauty of what God has done to bring us to this place. Our happiness then comes from the heart, and the more our hearts seek to know God, the more knowledge we receive and our hearts are happy.

If we want to have a menu of happy choices, then we must learn more about what it means to love, so that hate and its cronies all fade away. If we want to lift others up, we build their confidence and courage, leaving the words that bring destruction far behind. We keep choosing to be happy.

We wonder sometimes about what it means to be happy. We question how anyone can live in the world and still maintain a spirit of joy, a childlike faith.

> *Choose to feast on the beauty of God.*

The answer is that people are happy who have taken God at his word, trusting in him for the circumstances they don't understand.

It's a new day and the table is set.

QUIET THE WAVES

Lord, thank you for feeding me so well. Thank you for helping me make good choices. I choose to remain forever in your love, for that is the only thing that really makes me happy. Amen.

Don't Pretend to Love

Love should be shown without pretending. Hate evil,
and hold on to what is good. Love each other like the members
of your family. Be the best at showing honor to each other.

—Romans 12:9-10

None of us likes to be patronized or scammed. When we've been duped into a false hope, or even a false love, it isn't much fun.

Do we ever pretend love, though? Sadly, even the best of us fall into that less-than-loving trap from time to time. We do it when we strive to accept strangers that we find off-putting or to adjust to family members who are on a very different track than we are in the ways they handle life. We might pretend to love them more than actually loving them as Jesus would.

Our goal, though, is to love each other authentically, like family members that we adore. We want to honor and respect each other so much that we come together with a spirit of love and put wind in one another's sails. We want to give more than we receive and offer our hands and our hearts to act for the good of those around us.

We're not always aware of someone else's motives, but we are aware of our own. As much as possible, be ready to deliver the real thing. Love your neighbors as yourself.

> *B*e authentic in your love and actions for others.

Quiet the Waves

Lord, help me always be real and operate with full integrity around others. Help me honor you in the ways that I act in any given situation. Amen.

Going Against the Tide

But as for Noah, the Lord approved of him. These are Noah's
descendants. In his generation, Noah was a moral
and exemplary man; he walked with God.

—Genesis 6:8-9

This description of Noah is captivating. Noah was going against the tide of his own community. He was out of sync with his culture. In spite of what others did around him, he continued to do what he believed was right. He continued to behave in ways that were considered moral for his time and was a man of great integrity. He walked with God.

Not to be morbid, but that's quite an epitaph. What do you suppose Noah had that others of his day didn't understand? Why weren't more people on God's side?

We live in a world where it is easy to get drawn into the things that shut out the light, that deter us from following the path of good, that keep us numb, never realizing what we're giving up. We too could be corrupted, wasting away and losing God's favor—and we may not even realize it's happening.

We could, but fortunately, God is watching out for us. He has given us the key to his approval, and it's to have faith in his only Son.

Get in sync with God's will and live in hope.

He's also made a promise to us, to be with us till the end of time. We have the opportunity even now to live moral and exemplary lives and walk with God. Walk with him today.

QUIET THE WAVES

Lord, help me see your hand in all that I do. Let me walk with you in peace and in the light of your redeeming love. Amen.

Minding Your Own Business

*Aim to live quietly, mind your own business,
and earn your own living, just as I told you.*

—1 Thessalonians 4:11

It might sound a little harsh for you to be told to "mind your own business," but it's also wise counsel. Living quietly, going about your business, and earning your own living are certainly worthy goals. So what's your business?

Your profession aside, the rest of your business has to do with your heart and with perfecting your soul to reflect more of the divine Spirit. Your business is to keep growing, keep watching, and keep learning.

Thomas à Kempis offered us this thought, "A pure, simple, and steadfast spirit is not distracted by the number of things to be done, because it performs them all to the honor of God, and endeavors to be at rest from self-seeking."

Tend toward becoming more of the person God meant you to be.

Your work is cut out for you, and today is another gracious opportunity to see what you can do to earn the kind of living that pays off for others because you've grown in the spirit of truth and have so much more to give.

Don't be distracted from becoming who God wants you to be.

Go about your business with joy.

QUIET THE WAVES

Lord, thank you for being involved in my business. Help me to become all that you meant me to become and to live quietly and joyfully in you. Amen.

Got Plans? Take 'em up a Notch!

My plans aren't your plans, nor are your ways my ways, says the
LORD. Just as the heavens are higher than the earth, so are my
ways higher than your ways, and my plans than your plans.

—Isaiah 55:8-9

Making plans can seem like a simple enough act. You create your list for the day and make a vow to check off at least three things on it before evening. You get to number one, smooth sailing, looking like you'll be in port in just a few moments when suddenly the winds of change start blowing, and before you know it, you're totally off course.

Of course, it's good to make plans. It's just better to realize that your plans and God's plans may not come together. He is, after all, the Creator. He creates change as he sees it so that you accomplish what he has in mind. He may not cross off the things he wanted you to accomplish in a day, because he carries a life planner and checks your progress with that. You're here on a mission, and he wants to be sure you get things done.

As you look at your plans today, consider taking them up a notch. Start by planning to spend time with your Creator, getting his blessing for the things you'll accomplish today, things that you and he can do together.

Your mission today: spend extra time with God.

QUIET THE WAVES

Lord, thank you for having big plans for my life. Help me stay connected to you in a way that keeps the path clear for me to achieve the goals you have set for me. Amen.

The Spirit of Truth

If you love me, you will keep my commandments. I will ask the Father, and he will send another Companion, who will be with you forever. This Companion is the Spirit of Truth, whom the world can't receive because it neither sees him nor recognizes him. You know him, because he lives with you and will be with you.

—John 14:15-17

Truth, nothing but the truth, so help me God. That thing we swear in courtrooms is an elusive notion. Your truth may not be the same as someone else's. It doesn't mean one of you is right and one is wrong; it means there may well be separate truths.

When Jesus sent us the "Companion," who is the Spirit of Truth, he did so that we might know truth and be set free from the little prisons we slip into in our own minds. He didn't just lend us the Spirit of Truth, he gave us a lifelong companion who would live with us forever. You know him and you recognize him, because you received Jesus.

We live with the Spirit of Truth. We may or may not wish to always know the truth, because we sometimes prefer to bend it or shape it to fit what works best for us, but we have the option of seeking real truth. We have the opportunity always to replace our own thoughts with those that line up more precisely with the One who shares life with us all the time and knows us better than we know ourselves.

May truth prevail in all that you do today.

QUIET THE WAVES

Lord, thank you for your precious Spirit of Truth. Thank you for giving me the freedom to always tell the truth as your Spirit guides me. Amen.

This Thing Called Love

May the Lord cause you to increase and enrich your love for each other and for everyone in the same way as we also love you.

—1 Thessalonians 3:12

Love is such an awesome concept, it's often hard to define. Sure, we think we have a grasp of what it means to love. After all, we love our spouse and our children and others in our family. We have a reasonable sense of love.

But it may be time to turn up the heat. What would it take to increase your real understanding of love?

Like most things, love thrives on attention. In fact, it often demands attention. It grows with genuine interest and effort. It takes shape through good times and bad times. James Bryden said, "Love does not die easily. It is a living thing. It thrives in the face of all life's hazards, save one—neglect."

God is interested in how we experience love, and he does not want us to neglect it. His love for us is steady and strong, and he wants ours to be like that with others and with him.

Love is a living thing, and you and God share a love that is a match made in heaven.

Today, pour on the love everywhere you go.

QUIET THE WAVES

Lord, your love for me and others is beyond me, beyond my understanding. I know it's real, though, and I know that more than anything I want my love for others to grow. Please help me embrace all you want me to know about love. Amen.

The Strength of Gentleness

Be glad in the Lord always! Again I say, be glad! Let your gentleness show in your treatment of all people. The Lord is near.

—Philippians 4:4-5

Most of us really appreciate being around people who exude kindness and gentleness. We may wonder what it is they have that gives them the strength to be like that. We may marvel that they are so consistent in their mannerisms, so quietly confident in who they are. They treat everyone they meet as though they were lifelong friends. They're strong, and we admire them.

Those who are confident in who they are, who lead with integrity and fight the good fight, have no need to come out in a raging fury. They know that more can be accomplished for the good of all others by a gentle spirit. As it says in Proverbs 15, "A sensitive answer turns back wrath, but an offensive word stirs up anger."

May gentleness stir in your heart today, coming to your aid when someone is unkind, standing up for you when someone bruises your spirit, and guiding you when you can't quite find your way. May the gentleness of Jesus permeate your soul and fix itself on those who come into your midst. As you show them your gentle spirit, God will show them his.

> *Even in chaos, show a spirit of gentleness and love.*

QUIET THE WAVES

Lord, you so often deal gently with me. Help me keep my head around others today, giving them a gentle touch of love according to your will and purpose. Amen.

The Drink That Refreshes

*Both fresh water and salt water don't come
from the same spring, do they?*

—James 3:11

During winter months, we may love to dream about sandy beaches
and warm salty water. We imagine the sounds of seagulls and ocean
waves and shells along the shore. We love it until we need a nice cool
drink. Hmmm . . . imagine being surrounded by blissful breezes and
burning sands but with no cold refreshing drink. Everything is salt
water. It looks like water, sounds like water, but it can't refresh you
from the inside. It only leaves you feeling drier and thirstier.

Life can be like that. We don't notice whether we're being
nourished because for the moment we're being satisfied. Once the
illusion fades, we catch the reality like we just stepped on a jellyfish.
We are almost startled to realize we need a taste of something that
will truly sustain us, something more.

Your current faith may sustain you very well, or it may just keep you afloat on an endless sea of uncertainty. It may be time to drink more deeply and receive greater refreshment.

> *S*eek to drink from the satisfying Spirit of God.

There is a beautiful beach, a place where you can play and hang out in the sun. All you have to do is ask and you'll be there, filled forever with the cool, refreshing Spirit that will never leave you thirsty again.

QUIET THE WAVES

Lord, thank you for being the only living water that quenches the thirst of your children. Thank you for giving us all we need. Amen.

It All Begins with You

I was hungry and you gave me food to eat. I was thirsty and you gave me a drink. I was a stranger and you welcomed me.

—Matthew 25:35

It's easy in our culture to gloss over the needs of our neighbors and those who are still strangers to us in the world. We can pass by the homeless and imagine that they just weren't very good at managing their money or they really should join AA or some other "will somebody else please fix them" program. We may even give to United Way or some other such agency through the places we work. That makes giving so easy we don't even have to think about it. To us, it's just a loss of income anyway.

So how can we recognize the opportunity we have to act like Jesus? How will we differentiate the mindless-though-helpful giving from the kind that causes us to stop and notice what we're actually doing? When you give with a full intention, from the heart, isn't that more of the idea that Jesus had in mind?

Giving is always a choice. Whether you put your heart and mind into it is also a choice. Feeding others is not simply a matter of buying a meal. It's a function of inviting them to the feast of a gracious God who gave everything for our good.

Give from the heart with cheerful and loving intention.

Giving begins with you. It keeps you in the flow of blessing in ways that nothing can measure. Is anyone thirsty in your midst today? Be their blessing.

QUIET THE WAVES

Lord, show me how I can open up my heart and be more generous to others. I know that you have been more than generous to me. Amen.

Now That's a Mouthful!

Your speech should always be gracious and sprinkled with insight
so that you may know how to respond to every person.

—Colossians 4:6

You're speechless! Someone has just done something that surprised you and disappointed you so much, you hardly know what to say. Your first impulse is to charge in and make your appeal, let them know they crossed the line, totally messed things up, and yet . . . that isn't really the response God is looking for.

When you take a little time to breathe, to rethink the issue, you might be able to come up with a reasonable explanation for the incident, something that will give you a place to start in repairing the relationship before a major meltdown happens. You might be able to ease up on the resentments and see a glimpse of what God sees, even in this messy bit of drama. You can choose to be gracious, to take time to think through your response so that what you say can make a positive difference to the whole situation.

When you've been surprised by someone's actions or comments, it's not easy to do the right thing, and yet, God would have you try to do so. We're all still growing, and all we can do is thank

Think—pray—before responding to hurtful comments.

God that he gives us room to do so. Let's give each other that same space even when we're tempted to give out a mouthful.

QUIET THE WAVES

Lord, you know it isn't easy to be quiet when my feelings are hurt. Please help me remember your incredible kindness to me when I'm tempted to say more than is gracious to someone else. Amen.

Live Without Fear

You didn't receive a spirit of slavery to lead you back again into fear, but you received a Spirit that shows you are adopted as his children. With this Spirit, we cry, "Abba, Father."

—Romans 8:15

Do you ever feel less than thankful for a situation you find yourself in, situations that give rise to fear? Maybe your son just quit college without giving you a reason why, or you lost your job without any notice or severance. Maybe you just got diagnosed with a serious illness, or you've been told you won't be able to have a baby.

When everything feels topsy-turvy and you wonder what you're going to do next, the answer is simple. You're going to run to your Father in heaven and explain everything you know about the issue you face. Then you're going to thank him. You're going to thank him for helping work out a solution that's perfect for you. You're going to also thank him for his Spirit that he gives you so generously to help you in any situation.

Hang in there with God. He won't let you down, and he'll make sure you have what you need. Be thankful you have him to face whatever happens to you today.

*L*ook for comfort from the Holy Spirit during fearful times.

QUIET THE WAVES

Lord, thank you for being there with me no matter what happens today. I put all my worries, all my joys, all my heart and life into your merciful hands. Amen.

Simply Divine Conversation!

When all the people saw the column of cloud standing at the tent's entrance, they would all rise and then bow down at the entrances to their tents. In this way the Lord used to speak to Moses face-to-face, like two people talking to each other.

—Exodus 33:10-11

These days it's pretty easy to connect with the people you love. If you're near, you stop by. If you aren't, you get on the phone or you pull up Skype or a similar app and in a matter of moments you can be talking face to face. When we're talking to God, we might have a feeling that our prayers are more like getting on the phone. We may not always hear what God is saying from the other end, because if there's a bad connection, it's probably our system that is causing it.

We might wonder what it takes to have direct communication with God. We might ask ourselves why we're always in the fog. The truth is that even though it will be exciting when we're able to see each other clearly, we aren't at a loss; we aren't left without a way to be closely connected. We can always hear God if we're willing to listen for his tender voice. He speaks through others, he speaks through our intuitive understanding, he reaches out any way that he can to be sure we're connected to him and that we too are part of a divine conversation.

Join the conversation when God speaks to you.

QUIET THE WAVES

Lord, thank you for giving me a way to talk with you and to feel connected to you all the time. Thank you for giving me a clear signal that you are truly there with me today. Amen.

Pass on the Blessings

Finally, all of you be of one mind, sympathetic, lovers of your fellow believers, compassionate. . . . You were called to do this so that you might inherit a blessing.

—1 Peter 3:8-9

Someone needs what you have to give today. It may be a small gift of encouragement through your words or your greetings. It may be a gentle heart that listens with compassion. It may be your clever sense of humor and your ability to chase away the clouds of gloom that threaten their day. You are God's hands and feet, his eyes and ears.

Emily Dickinson reflected on this need in her own way when she wrote the following:

> *They might not need me; but they might.*
> *I'll let my head be just in sight;*
> *A smile as small as mine might be*
> *Precisely their necessity.*

Your smile, your thoughts, your helping hands are just what somebody else needs today. Bless others and God will immediately bless you. Show his face and shine his light everywhere you go today. You are blessed to be a blessing.

Show someone kindness, gentleness, and encouragement today.

QUIET THE WAVES

Lord, you know the needs of each person I will encounter today. Help me see them as you see them. Help me offer them the gift of your blessing. Amen.

Is That a Gray Hair?

I am the one, and until you turn gray
I will support you. I have done it, and I will continue to bear it;
I will support and I will rescue.

—Isaiah 46:4

∼⌒∽

If you're of a certain age, you probably remember the first gray hair. You were startled, annoyed at its presence, ready to immediately pull it out. After all, you're far too young for that.

If the hair-dye manufacturers have their way, you won't have to worry about those telling gray hairs. You can cover them up and no one will know. Okay . . . God will know.

This brings the realization that God has been with you since before you were born, watched over you relentlessly like a mother hen, and will never see you as anything but his child to care for and support. He will keep his end of the bargain until he has you safely tucked back into his arms.

Today, whatever you might be doing, stop and really think about what it means that God sees you right now. The God who created the whole universe, set the stars in motion, and made the mountains and the ocean, that same God sees you right where you stand. Reach out to him and thank him for all he has done to keep

Since before your birth, God has had plans of provision.

you safe and to let his face shine upon you. Remember too that he knows every hair on your head, the gray ones too, and even if you had no hair at all, he'd still see you as his beloved child.

QUIET THE WAVES

Lord, thanks for knowing all that I will be going through today. Bless my work and my family and those I love in Jesus's name. Amen.

Buzz! Thank You for Playing!

I fight like a boxer in the ring, not like someone who is shadowboxing. Rather I'm landing punches on my own body and subduing it like a slave. I do this to be sure that I myself won't be disqualified after preaching to others.

—1 Corinthians 9:26-27

Whether you think of it this way or not, every day you step into the ring. You take on the opponents who are out there ready to punch you, take you out, discourage you, and keep you down. It takes a lot of accurate movement of your feet and a few indirect hits to keep standing. As you prepare to get into the match, you have to have a lot of self-discipline. That's where the work really is. That's where you have to learn to stand.

It's up to us to be disciplined in our daily routines enough that when something blindsides us or knocks us for a loop, we can stand back up again and keep going. One way we protect ourselves is by putting on the full armor of God. We get that armor by staying entrenched with our Creator, stuck to the Word like it's our last avenue of defense, holding on to it for dear life.

> *T*rain yourself to do what is right in God's sight.

God is with you as you enter the arena, even more as you step into the ring. He will guide your steps, give you strength, and keep you standing according to his grace and mercy. Give him thanks and praise.

QUIET THE WAVES

Lord, thanks for being with me in the daily battles, the moments when I'm not always prepared for what comes next. Help me stay close by your side today. Amen.

Wow! That Was Stupid!

Patience leads to abundant understanding,
but impatience leads to stupid mistakes.

—Proverbs 14:29

You have goals for yourself. But what happens if things take a little longer than you expected? What happens to your faith when you have to wait things out?

We live in a world of instant gratification. When the internet goes down for five minutes, we're irritated. We're used to getting information now, and we don't like it very much when we have to wait . . . for anything!

Look at what happens if you get caught in a traffic jam for fifteen minutes, or you're in line at the grocery store with the sweet little lady who has twenty-seven coupons. At first, you're a little annoyed, maybe a little antsy, and then just out-and-out angry because someone else is taking up your precious time. After all, you're pretty important and you have things to do.

Impatience leads to all kinds of problems. You try to go around the traffic jam, only to get caught in even greater congestion elsewhere. Today, watch the flow and energy around you.

*P*ractice patience today to receive abundant rewards.

Observe your willingness to slow down enough to recognize that prayerful patience will reap greater rewards. The reward will surely help limit those stupid mistakes.

QUIET THE WAVES

Lord, I know that I am not always patient. Help me realize that you can use me a lot more when I slow down and think of you. Amen.

It's Black and White

Anyone who tries to keep all of the Law but fails at
one point is guilty of failing to keep all of it.

—James 2:10

There are few things in this world that truly are black or white. According to James, the fact that breaking the law makes a person guilty of breaking the whole law is one of those things. We might be able to say we kept nine Commandments, but the one we missed out on throws us into the realm of breaking the whole law.

If you've ever tried to keep one of the Commandments for even a day, you can quickly see how easily they are broken and how difficult it really is to achieve salvation through them. The Ten Commandments then are the perfect guides to why we need Jesus. With him, we are rescued from the dilemma. With him, we are saved from the law, because there is a new law in our hearts that he alone can put there. We are saved, pure and simple . . . black and white.

Today, give Jesus your heart, your mind, and your soul, and thank him for helping you work out your salvation through his rescue efforts on your behalf.

> *K*now that you are saved through Christ's death and resurrection.

QUIET THE WAVES

Lord, help me remember that I can't survive in this world or the next without you. You're my only redeemer and friend. I praise you and thank you. Amen.

Getting Through the SATs!

Dear friends, don't be surprised about the fiery trials
that have come among you to test you. These are not strange
happenings. Instead, rejoice as you share Christ's suffering.
You share his suffering now so that you may also have
overwhelming joy when his glory is revealed.

—1 Peter 4:12-13

Remember when you were getting ready to leave high school and you had to take the SATs? That was the big test that colleges would use to get a sense of your readiness to perform well in college. It was also a screening tool that they could use to advise you about what the best direction might be for your life.

Welcome to life's SATs! You're always going to have more tests to take no matter how far away from school you get. We might call the ones you're going through now Suffering and Training—at least that's how some of those tests feel. We might call them Spiritual

Activity Training. Those would be the ones that remind you to plug in a little more often to the One who made you. He brought you here, and he sticks with you till you get back to him, so a little training helps you both gauge how things are going.

> *C*elebrate trials knowing that indescribable joy awaits you in the future.

Whatever is going on, know that in faith you already passed with flying colors, and one day you'll be overwhelmed with joy as you see your Father standing ready to applaud your hard work and give you a diploma.

QUIET THE WAVES

Lord, sometimes I do feel like I'm still being tested. I guess you're working with me to help me graduate with flying colors. Thanks for being there through every test I have to take. Amen.

You Have an Inheritance Right Now!

The Holy Spirit is the down payment on our inheritance,
which is applied toward our redemption as God's own people,
resulting in the honor of God's glory.

—Ephesians 1:14

The day you recognized that you were a child of a loving Father, when you chose to bear his name and his resemblance to the rest of the world, you were given an inheritance. He left you a portion to make your life a bit easier right now. He gave you a down payment in the form of the Holy Spirit.

What does it mean to have free access to God's Spirit? How does that help you right now? J. B. Phillips said, "Every time we say, 'I believe in the Holy Spirit,' we mean that we believe that there is a living God able and willing to enter a human personality and change it."

That's not the end of our inheritance, though. The Holy Spirit also dispenses gifts to us. They are gifts to help us live our lives in the best ways, able to accomplish the tasks at hand. He offers gifts like kindness and goodness and self-control. He directs our steps as long as we're willing to walk with him.

Spend your inheritance wisely and joyfully. It is the Father's gift to you today.

You are a child of God, an heir to abundant gifts of the Holy Spirit.

QUIET THE WAVES

Lord, you have freely loved and freely given so much to me. Please give me the wisdom to share my rich inheritance with others according to your will and purpose. Amen.

Life in the Spirit, the Spirit in Life

But you aren't self-centered. Instead you are in the Spirit,
if in fact God's Spirit lives in you. If anyone doesn't have the
Spirit of Christ, they don't belong to him. If Christ is in you,
the Spirit is your life because of God's righteousness,
but the body is dead because of sin.

—Romans 8:9-10

If you're off center, that's a good thing. In your life with Christ, you aren't intended to be in the center; He is! He is your engine, your power, the thruster that gets you into the day. He's your, pardon the expression, Holy Smoke!

When you're in the Spirit, you're on fire for God. You may remember that holy fire from when you were first baptized in the Spirit. It was almost overwhelming to have that sense that you were somehow connected to the Creator of the universe. It was more joy than you knew what to do with and made you want to tell everybody about your faith. You may have even been somewhat obnoxious about it.

That fire may have cooled some by now, maturing with you into more of a peaceful flame, an eternal flame that will never be extinguished. It's good to get to where you are now, not only off

> *B*laze with the holy fire of the Spirit even as you continue to mature in faith.

center, but pleased to be so. Your life is given over to the Spirit, and you couldn't be happier. Now, doesn't that just make every new day more exciting?

QUIET THE WAVES

Lord, I remember when we first met and how in love I was. It was a great feeling, but the relationship we share now feels even better, steady and more whole. Thanks for giving me the Spirit. Amen.

Putting a Lid on Anger

Fools show all their anger, but the wise hold it back.

—Proverbs 29:11

Henry Drummond had some colorful insights to share about anger. He said, "No form of vice, not worldliness, not greed of gold, not drunkenness itself, does more to un-Christianize society than evil temper. For embittering life, for breaking up communities, for destroying the most sacred relationships, for devastating homes, for withering up men and women, for taking the bloom off childhood; in short, for sheer gratuitous misery-producing power, this influence stands alone."

There is, of course, a righteous anger, like the kind Jesus demonstrated in the temple with the money changers. There is a time to stand up, perhaps in anger, when injustice rears its head in any form. On this side of things, Martin Luther said, "I never work better than when I am inspired by anger; for when I am angry, I can write, pray, and preach well, for then my whole temperament is quickened, my understanding sharpened, and all mundane vexations and temptations depart."

Just be aware of the things that trigger an angry response. Understand whether your motivation is to teach or destroy, to drive a point or to drive

> *Let your anger lead you to make a better life for those around you.*

someone away. In any case, remember to not let the sun go down on your anger today.

QUIET THE WAVES

Lord, help me use the emotion of anger only when it will help create positive change. Amen.

Authorization Code, Please!

A huge storm arose on the lake so that waves were
sloshing over the boat. But Jesus was asleep. They came
and woke him, saying, "Lord, rescue us! We're going to drown!"
He said to them, "Why are you afraid, you people of
weak faith?" Then he got up and gave orders to the winds
and the lake, and there was a great calm.

—Matthew 8:24-26

We've become pretty skeptical about any voice of authority because those who have that voice often abuse their power. So what about Jesus? What shall we say in this day and age about his authority?

Matthew 28:18 quotes Jesus as saying, "I've received all authority in heaven and on earth." That's why we can believe that even now, he can speak to and for us. We can trust in his authority.

We all have days when we feel like we're drowning. We're drowning in paperwork or caving in to worry or overwhelmed by grief. We have something that sends the winds and waves crashing over us just as surely as if we were in a rocky boat. We can't calm things down on our own. We need someone who can find the right code to address our problem and authorize a change. That is why we need Jesus!

> *Call on Jesus when you're overwhelmed with what life tosses your way.*

As you walk through today, whether you stand firm or have shaky knees, remember that you have a solid place to stand because you live and breathe and stand on the authority of God's only Son!

QUIET THE WAVES

Lord, thank you for taking the guesswork out of my hands. Thank you for being the One I can turn to for anything I need. Amen.

You've Got a Friend!

I don't call you servants any longer, because servants don't know
what their master is doing. Instead, I call you friends, because
everything I heard from my Father I have made known to you.

—John 15:15

You've got a lot of relationships. You've got family, coworkers, bosses perhaps, and church acquaintances—lots of people in your life. The best relationships, though, are the ones you attach to the word *friend*.

Authentic friendships are those you count on when life is going haywire, or those that bring you a laugh when you can't step outside your troubles long enough to find one on your own. These are the friends who will tell you when you're acting weird or who will love you when you're a bit crazy. They'll hold your hand in the middle of the night and walk with you through a scary surgery. These are your friends.

If we think about it, it's amazing that God would want to call us his friends. After all, that assumes a give-and-take relationship. That assumes we're there for him just like he's there for us. It also assumes trust and joy and depth of experience.

You have a friend in Jesus; talk to him, listen to him.

Today, think about your friendship with God. What do you have to give him? What do you think would make your friendship stronger? You and God are friends. You're on a first-name basis. Spend a little time with him. He'd love to hear from you.

QUIET THE WAVES

Lord, thank you for inviting me to be your friend. Help me be a better friend to you all the time. Amen.

Might, Wisdom, and Knowledge

But God made the earth by his might; he shaped the world
by his wisdom, crafted the skies by his knowledge.
At the sound of his voice, the heavenly waters roar.
He raises the clouds from the ends of the earth. He sends
the lightning with the rain, the wind from his treasuries.

—Jeremiah 10:12-13

God shaped the world as we know it through his own inexhaustible powers of wisdom and knowledge and might. He set the clouds in the skies and spoke the rains and the mists into being. He has powers that are without peer in this universe. Yet, even so, Jesus came along many years after the prophet Jeremiah and reminded us that this God who made all things seeks a relationship with his creation, his children. It is by faith in this same God that we are told we too can come to wisdom and knowledge to do in part the things he has done.

Knowledge can be attained by much practice and study. Wisdom must partner with faithfulness in order to lead with strength and honor. Most of us strive to attain more knowledge and to lead our lives with more wisdom. Yet, one thing may still elude us. We may not discover more of what faithfulness offers.

> *S*eek a deeper relationship with God, the source of all knowledge and wisdom.

May God grant you wisdom today as you seek to know more of him and all that he wants for your life.

QUIET THE WAVES

Lord, you are the source of all wisdom and knowledge and through your might, you created all that we see. Help me delight in your creation and learn all that I can about you as a matter of love and faithfulness. Amen.

God Had Choices

While we were still weak, at the right moment, Christ died for
ungodly people. It isn't often that someone will die for
a righteous person, though maybe someone might dare to die for
a good person. But God shows his love for us, because
while we were still sinners Christ died for us.

—Romans 5:6-8

God had choices. He could have scratched all his plans and said he was done with us. After all, he tried twice and the human race still didn't seem to get it. We're still pathetic and selfish and pretty hard to live with most of the time. Yet, even with choices, even after the flood, God felt so bad for what he had done, and for us, that he gave us a rainbow as a promise that life would go on.

Fortunately for the human race, God made a plan. He looked at us one more time, and with more love than we could ever possibly earn or deserve, he sent an innocent baby boy to be our sacrifice. The

Lamb of God, Jesus, would live among us, laugh with us, cry with us, and work with us and yet know that he would one day lay down his life so that we could live.

God didn't have to do it. He had choices. His decision was made a long time ago and it still stands. He won't change his mind. We're his lost sheep and he was mighty glad to send us a Shepherd.

Choose to love someone today who appears unloveable.

QUIET THE WAVES

Lord, I don't know how to thank you for making it possible for me to come back to live with you someday, but I do. Thank you for loving me more than I can understand. Amen.

Waiting for Forever!

With the Lord a single day is like a thousand years
and a thousand years are like a single day. The Lord
isn't slow to keep his promise, as some think of slowness,
but he is patient toward you.

—2 Peter 3:8-9

When you were a kid, it seemed time went so slowly. You waited for Christmas and your birthday and the big vacation with the family. Now that you're a little older, days and nights may seem to melt into each other and make you wonder how anything can get done when there is so little time.

Peter reminds us essentially that with God time is not really an issue. In fact, he invented the whole concept of time, and it appears that he had no limitations for himself. But for us time is a mystery.

The thing we have to notice is what happens to our patience or our ability to wait when time drags on. When everything about life is suddenly grounded and nothing moves, when everything stops, then you might feel somewhat dismayed.

Today, pay closer attention to your time and how you spend it. How much of it did you dedicate to God?

*P*ause from your busy day and spend more time with God.

QUIET THE WAVES

Lord, I admit that I get frustrated by time. I either don't have enough of it, or I have a little too much on my hands, and then I get impatient. Remind me that you are the authority of my time, the One who knows how I best need to live my life. Amen.

Don't Get Hooked!

A sensitive answer turns back wrath, but an offensive word
stirs up anger. The tongue of the wise enhances knowledge,
but the mouth of a fool gushes with stupidity.

—Proverbs 15:1-2

An old adage reminds us that a fish only gets caught when its mouth is open. The same might be said of us. Sometimes the best thing we can do is keep our mouths shut. Not as easy as it sounds, is it?

It's one thing to give advice when someone asks us for it, or to give a response when a question has been directed our way, but sometimes we jump into an opportunity to give our not-so-humble opinion before a request was made. When we do that, we may give valuable advice, but many times we have our own agenda for the response we give, and so we're not really much help.

A rule of thumb might be this: Don't give advice unless someone asks you directly for it. Then, don't give advice unless the two of you have spent some time in prayer, taking the situation to your heavenly Father so that what you then discuss is part of his design, removing personal agendas and bringing clarity to the situation.

Today and every day, seek God's advice first.

QUIET THE WAVES

Lord, I admit that I get caught in other people's drama. I try to fix things that aren't mine to fix. Please help me always seek wisdom from you before I offer my thoughts to anyone else. Amen.

For God so Loved You

God so loved the world that he gave his only Son,
so that everyone who believes in him won't perish
but will have eternal life.

—John 3:16

Can you really take that in? Are you able to comprehend what it actually means that the God of the universe, the One who created everything and who has the only real power and authority over heaven and earth, actually loves you? Wow! Who are you?

Who you are may not be nearly as important as what you are. You are his child, his object of affection. You are the one he sent his only Son to redeem because he couldn't stand the thought that anything would ever happen to you. You mean the world to God, and he is doing everything he can to prove himself to you.

Today, take a moment and imagine what it really means to be loved by God. Embrace the idea. Pray and ask God to help you understand it more fully. Then remind yourself that such love deserves to be shared. You're in a relationship, and it's the biggest one that you'll ever be part of. It's bigger than your spouse, it's bigger than your partnership at the firm or your membership in the church. It's you andGod, one to one.

Imagine: God loves you so much he sacrificed his Son in order to save you!

God so loved you that he acted on your behalf a long time ago. You have every opportunity to act on God's behalf today.

QUIET THE WAVES

Lord, I can hardly take in the idea of your great love. I know that it is a gift of your spirit, and I treasure it. Help me to be worthy of your love in all that I do. Amen.

What Motivates You to Do Good?

Let us consider each other carefully for the purpose
of sparking love and good deeds.

—Hebrews 10:24

Most of us want to do good things. We are interested in the well-being of others and are motivated in that interest in a variety of ways and for a host of reasons. For some, doing good comes naturally. Compassion and empathy motivate our spirits. God's love then pushes us to do even more.

For others, a sense of social activism drives the desire to take on humanity and do good deeds. Some of us feel compelled to do good things because of our social position or status in a community. We do good, but our hearts are not necessarily in it.

What makes the difference? The key is to see if any of the motivation for what we do comes from love. How much do you have to think about the good things you do? How much do you expect in return? How much publicity and ego-boosting do you want from the things you do?

Let us choose to do good in any way that we can for those in our midst today.

 et God's love motivate you to pass on that love.

QUIET THE WAVES

Lord, there are people in real need all around me. Help me love them enough to do what I can simply because you have made it possible for me to act and because of my love for you. Amen.

Because of the Cross

But as for me, God forbid that I should boast about
anything except for the cross of our Lord Jesus Christ.
The world has been crucified to me through him,
and I have been crucified to the world.

—Galatians 6:14

Thomas à Kempis suggested that you "carry the cross patiently, and with perfect submission, and in the end it will carry you." We can wear a cross around our necks, admire a cross in a beautiful cathedral, imagine the three crosses on the hill of Calvary, but none of those images will serve to substitute for what our hearts must understand about the cross of Christ.

Submitting to the cross means you're unique. You're known by the God of the universe and by Jesus. You're in the world, but not of the world, able to bring something to it that couldn't have ever happened without the events on Calvary.

M. Lloyd-Jones wrote, "The preaching of the cross of Christ was the very center and heart of the message of the apostles, and there is nothing I know of that is more important than that."

Remember you were bought with a price.

The Good Friday message that leads to Easter is made new every time you remember what God has done to bring you back to himself. You inspired him to give his only Son so that you might live in relationship to him. Today and every day, live your life as a person who is highly aware of being redeemed.

QUIET THE WAVES

Lord, I thank you for loving me more than I can even comprehend. I thank you for redeeming my soul. Amen.

Your Inner Beauty

You are the one who created my innermost parts; you knit me
together while I was still in my mother's womb.
I give thanks to you that I was marvelously set apart.
Your works are wonderful—I know that very well.

—Psalm 139:13-14

You are wonderful! You are the divine craftsmanship of an expert. You are the best version of you that there could be. How is that possible? Because you were divinely inspired, and God knew you before you were ever born.

You're God's masterpiece and nothing can change that. You were and are marvelously set apart.

What does that mean to you? It means turn up your light and let your inner self, your beautiful self, lead the way and live for him as though living is the only mission you have on earth. Live as though what you do is important to God because it is. What you do matters. What you think and believe and dream matters. God sees you and he loves you from the inside out, and he wants your life to be filled with creative endeavors that bring his loving kingdom to your family, your neighbors, and those beyond.

> *A*s God's creation, you are called to be creative with your life.

QUIET THE WAVES

Lord, I know you formed me and loved me before I was even a light in my mother's eyes. Help me take that in and realize how important I am to you. Help me shine from the place of my innermost being and bring your light to those around me. Amen.

Faithful over a Little

*His master replied, "Excellent! You are a good and faithful
servant! You've been faithful over a little. I'll put you in charge
of much. Come, celebrate with me."*

—Matthew 25:21

Most of us are never going to be in a position of great power or
influence. We won't command armies or rule over thousands of
people. We're simply going to be everyday, ordinary people who now
and then do extraordinary things. The key to any of it is locked into
our level of faithfulness.

You have a job to do, a mission of sorts, a definite purpose.
You're continually being put into situations that bring out the best
of your talents and cause you to fulfill your mission. You are always
guided to the goal of getting your job done.

How much are you willing to do to answer the call you have
been given? God is always faithful to you. He is always on the job

and never slumbers or sleeps, never takes a day off, never unplugs the phone. He is faithful.

It stands to reason then that he wants his children to be faithful too. He wants us to be faithful in little things so he can give us the opportunity to grow in faith and take on even bigger things.

Go and serve the Lord, fulfilling his purpose in your life.

Remember that God is best served by you when you desire to be more for him, when you desire to have a bigger faith.

QUIET THE WAVES

Lord, I love the way you help me to learn more of the work you want me to do. Help me always be faithful to the tasks that you give me, in big ways and small ways. Amen.

The Problem . . . with Love

We even take pride in our problems, because we know
that trouble produces endurance, endurance produces
character, and character produces hope.

—Romans 5:3-4

The truth is this. Love is not the problem, it's the solution. Certainly soap operas and Harlequin romances carry on about the problem of love, but maybe love isn't the problem at all. Maybe if we handle any problem with love, the right kind and degree of love, we have reason to hope.

Hope keeps us going and growing. When we show our willingness to endure the hard things, to grow past fears and obstacles, and to keep our eyes on the One who can change things, it makes a difference. Handling a problem with love instead of fear brings us into the place where change is possible. It brings us face to face with the Holy Spirit, who can then intercede for us and bring us back to safety and peace.

It's been said that "the will of God will never take you where the grace of God cannot keep you." You can handle your problems with despair, or you can handle your problems with God's love.

Fill your heart with hope as you seek every solution through love!

QUIET THE WAVES

Lord, I don't always know how to tap into your love. I try hard to do anything I can to fix a problem, and then I come to you exhausted and weary. Help me come to you first and fill me with hope. Amen.

Under Constant Construction

*Every house is built by someone, but God
is the builder of everything.*

—Hebrews 3:4

If you stand in front of the Taj Mahal or Buckingham Palace or even the White House, it's easy to be awed by the architecture and the intricate design. It's awesome to imagine the one who conceived that design, created the blueprints, and made it come to life. It's an amazing and awesome work of art.

When you reflect on the joy you get from the home you've chosen to live in or perhaps the dream home you hope one day to have, remember that whoever designed the house was inspired by the same Source that inspires everything you do each day.

There is only one builder of all things and that is God. He sees what you need, and he constructs the best possible way for it to work out. He creates all the blueprints and someone else builds on his design.

As you stand in front of your own front door, your own little "White House," remember the Builder. Remember the One who wants to be the head of your house, the one who built in some very special options just for you. It may well be under construction, but that's okay. God is willing to redesign as you understand more fully what making a home with him is all about.

> *W*ith quiet assurance, build your life on the foundation of Jesus Christ.

QUIET THE WAVES

Lord, thank you for building a house that is so warm and inviting. Thanks for working on it with me to create it in a way that fulfills your purpose for my life. Amen.

A Matter of the Heart

The one who searches hearts knows how the Spirit thinks,
because he pleads for the saints, consistent with God's will.

—Romans 8:27

You probably don't think of yourself as a "saint," but in the bigger picture, you are, because you are a redeemed child of God, and you have the Spirit of Jesus within you. That Spirit is the one who prays for you, keeping you connected to God in every way, working tirelessly for your good. Isn't it wonderful to have such an advocate always in your corner?

Your connection with God is a matter of the heart. It's a relationship that only you and he can share—the most significant relationship of your life. When your heart is aligned with the will of God, you can make a difference in the world; you can do good in the name of Jesus, and you are a saint. Watch your motives, the reasons behind the things you do for good. Those that come truly from your heart are the ones you do by God's will.

We may not understand how the Spirit of God thinks; yet, we are beloved and protected, watched over by God himself so that we have the strength and the opportunity to do good and to

*A*lign your heart with God's will to bring about his kingdom.

enrich the work of his kingdom. Open your heart even more to him today.

QUIET THE WAVES

Lord, thank you for taking care of me even when I'm not conscious of the work of your Spirit. Help me always align my life and my intentions with your will. Amen.

Flim-Flam Faith

*Be careful that you don't practice your religion in front of
people to draw their attention. If you do, you will have
no reward from your Father who is in heaven.*

—Matthew 6:1

You know about the flim-flam man? He's the one who shows up like the Music Man, shouting and gathering crowds, defining trouble with a capital T. He addresses an audience simply to take hold of their thinking and to get them to dig down deeper into their pockets. He's not just defining trouble, he is trouble.

Some apostles of faith today can be like that. There are some who attract huge crowds, pandering with their message, creating opportunity for dramatic events and getting people to give more of their hard-earned pensions. They're the flim-flam masters of faith. They may have started out with an honest hope of spreading the gospel, but they ended up only spreading their own fame.

God doesn't want a show. He doesn't want more drama. He's got enough of that to contend with in the world. What he wants is you with a sincere and devout heart, coming to him in prayer with thanksgiving. He wants your love and your integrity; and if you witness for him, he wants you to do it from the abundance of faith that flows through your veins.

Let your actions be motivated at all times with love.

QUIET THE WAVES

Lord, I've never been particularly showy about my faith, but I'm a little turned off by those people who are. Help me to express my faith honestly in front of you and other people. Amen.

Have No Fear

*God didn't give us a spirit that is timid but one
that is powerful, loving, and self-controlled.*

—2 Timothy 1:7

The truth is that sometimes we're afraid we'll succeed. If we succeed
at something we've been putting off and telling others for years we
just couldn't do, then what happens? Our excuses are gone, and we
have to go about inventing some new ones.

We all have fears, and some of them are grounded and some
aren't, and it probably would do us good to figure out the differences.
Some people fear God himself. Pascal noted that "there is a virtuous
fear which is the effect of faith, and a vicious fear which is the product
of doubt and distrust. Persons of the one character fear to lose God;
those of the other character fear to find Him."

Whatever your fears are, God did not give you a spirit of
timidity. He did not put you in the world to be a wallflower hiding

behind every shadowy tree wondering what might be lurking beyond. He made you a brave soul! He gave you strength and power and the ability to discern when to act and when to simply walk on.

Face today with a spirit of calmness, hope, and love.

Remember that you have not been left defenseless. You've been given the power to achieve your goals. Have no fear, God is with you.

QUIET THE WAVES

Lord, please remind me that I don't do anything ever without you being part of it. Give me the strength I need to overcome the small obstacles of fear that would keep me stuck. Amen.

How Not to Please God!

There are six things that the Lord hates, seven things
detestable to him: snobbish eyes, a lying tongue,
hands that spill innocent blood, a heart set on wicked plans,
feet that run quickly to evil, a false witness who breathes lies,
and one who causes conflicts among relatives.

—Proverbs 6:16-19

You probably prefer to please God in the manner by which you address life and the people you know. Well, this proverb directs your attention to what you can do to NOT please God. Of course, none of these apply to you, but let's look again at one and see if you note any shades of similarity.

It may not occur to you that you could be snobbish in any way, but anything that separates us from having compassion for another human being may well hit this chord. Like Jesus's disciples who argued over who could sit next to him when he came into his kingdom, you may unconsciously elevate yourself in ways that bring snobbish eyes into play.

We are all apt to NOT please God on any given day with the things we do or say. We're not so perfectly adjusted to this world that we know how to sidestep the evils no matter how little

> *P*lease God by having compassion on everyone you meet today.

they might seem. Today, though, is a new day and a chance to offer God our best.

QUIET THE WAVES

Lord, I know that I'm as guilty as anyone of doing things that do not please you. Help me take quick note of those moments and realign myself with you and your love. Thank you for loving me just as I am. Amen.

Rooted in Faith

But now he has reconciled you by his physical body through death, to present you before God as a people who are holy, faultless, and without blame. But you need to remain well established and rooted in faith and not shift away from the hope given in the good news that you heard.

—Colossians 1:22-23

Are you aware of the way the aspens in Colorado are rooted to each other underground? They are literally all connected, holding on to one another and helping one another to sustain life because of their incredible root system.

What difference might there be if human beings were as rooted to one another as the aspens? What if we were then that deeply rooted to our faith in God?

Some roots run so deep you can hardly dig them out with heavy-duty machinery. Some pull out without any effort at all.

It can be a matter of not being rooted in the right kind of soil. If you're rooted in the soil of faith, held in place by the community you experience with other believers, then it will be much more difficult for the adversary to pull you away. God will hold on to you all your life because of his great love.

> *G*et back to your roots and let the Gardener take care of you.

QUIET THE WAVES

Lord, thank you for everything you do to nurture my faith, to protect me, and to keep me rooted in your love. Help me keep growing in you. Amen.

The Eyes of Faith

We live by faith and not by sight.

—2 Corinthians 5:7

Edward Teller is known for this wise saying: "When you get to the end of all the light you know and it's time to step into the darkness of the unknown, faith is knowing that one of two things will happen: either you will be given something solid to stand on, or you will be taught how to fly."

Sometimes your steps are uncertain. You feel like you're walking in the dark and waiting for God to give you a flashlight. Like a person in dense fog, you progress, get to the next spot, and notice that you can actually see just a little bit of the road ahead. You walk in the fog with faith.

When we're blinded by the fog that life can sometimes bring, it helps to remember these words from Helen Keller: "If the blind put their hand in God's, they find their way more surely than those who see but have not faith nor purpose."

God wants to walk with you and be your vision, your sight. He alone knows the path so well that he can keep your feet from stumbling. Today as you step into the world, ask him to come alongside you, to direct your steps, and to be your eyes.

> *W*alk with the eyes of faith, knowing your Father guides each step.

QUIET THE WAVES

Lord, be with me today as I go about my business. Sometimes I think I know exactly where I'm going, and sometimes I don't. Either way, I want to put my life in your hands, safe in faith. Amen.

The Place Where You Stand

Moses said, "I'm here." Then the Lord said,
"Don't come any closer! Take off your sandals,
because you are standing on holy ground."

—Exodus 3:4-5

How do we come into God's presence? How often do we recognize the place where we stand—when we talk to him, when we say our prayers, when we express our faith and our belief—as a holy space?

God's request was simple, yet it required one thing of Moses. It meant that he had to listen and obey. It meant that he had to understand that this was indeed an important moment in their relationship, for God was inviting Moses into his inner circle. It connected Moses most directly to the earth and perhaps gave him a way to feel God's presence even more.

We're not always inclined to remember God's holiness on a conscious level. We may not think of our conversations with him as taking place on holy ground, and yet that is where we stand every time we approach him with a humble heart, with a desire to get closer to him, with an understanding of our own humanity. God is holy.

Set apart time today to rest in his holy presence.

QUIET THE WAVES

Lord, I thank you for loving me so much that you're willing to let me share your friendship and be part of your inner circle. Help me be worthy of your love today and be mindful of those places that are holy and set apart unto you. Amen.

We Are Family

Keep loving each other like family. Don't neglect to open up
your homes to guests, because by doing this some have been
hosts to angels without knowing it.

—Hebrews 13:1-2

You may not have the same last name or the same address, but the writer of Hebrews encourages you to treat everyone who comes to visit or stay the night as family. Opening your heart and home to honored guests changes the dynamic of your relationship instantly. You create an atmosphere where everyone under your roof is your family.

What's so good about that? For one thing, you get to have authentic experience. You get to be yourself and your guest does too. You get to share your personal stories, your faith stories, and other matters in ways that resonate with truth and create opportunities for further discussion. You talk about things in a family that you can't begin to discuss with strangers.

You may not find yourself in the presence of angels, or then again, you may, but the point is to treat everyone like family. In fact, if you treat people with love, you'll be serving them as an angel of friendship, fellowship, and joy. Nothing could make your Father happier than to see you treat his other children so well.

Treat guests as if they were part of a loving family.

QUIET THE WAVES

Lord, help me always be a warm and generous host to anyone who finds their way to my door. As you have so lovingly welcomed me into your family, let me return the favor by the way I embrace those who spend time in my home. Amen.

Flashlight, Please!

Without guidance, a people will fall, but there is
victory with many counselors.

—Proverbs 11:14

When you have to walk down a dark street at night, it helps to have a flashlight. It may not give a lot of light to the situation, but it gives enough to keep you from falling into potholes.

Sometimes your flashlight comes in the form of other people. They speak with a voice of authority that feels like God himself must have put them directly onto your path. You may not have expected them, but God knew your need and so they rushed in and kept you on your feet. He knew adding their beam to yours could make all the difference.

Take a look around today for people in your life with energy-efficient "flashlights" who can help you move on to be victorious over whatever is lurking in the shadows. With a little help, you'll eventually move again into a faith that says, "Lord, I'm going to walk today totally trusting you, and I don't even need a flashlight."

Between his Word acting as a lamp to guide your feet and your faith to keep you moving forward, you'll be on your way rejoicing. It's going to be a great day!

Listen to the wise counselors who guide you into deeper faith.

QUIET THE WAVES

Lord, thank you for sending others to me to help guide my way. Thanks for being the light of my life. Amen.

Getting Things Right!

In those days there was no king in Israel;
each person did what they thought to be right.

—Judges 17:6

Now this is an interesting thought. What if we all just did what feels right to us without any regard for what is right for someone else? What happens when there are no rules?

When Moses left his people and went up on the mountain to talk with God, they got bored waiting for him. When they got bored, they started thinking maybe they knew best how to handle things. Without any rules, they all just did what they thought was right, and it didn't work out well. God sent Moses back down the mountain with the rules, posthaste.

Most of us resist rules a little bit. Yet, the best thing for any of us is to know the boundaries, to understand the limits. Moses gave us the Ten Commandments and that helped establish how God wanted things to be done. Jesus gave us the two rules of love: love God and love your neighbor. When we follow God's rules, we have a little better chance of getting things right.

> *R*ules to live by:
> love God and
> love your neighbor.

QUIET THE WAVES

Lord, thank you for setting boundaries, reminding me of the important things so that when I choose to make or break a rule, I know I am measuring it against your rules that have everything to do with love. Amen.

When Nothing Fits

Don't be conformed to the patterns of this world,
but be transformed by the renewing of your minds
so that you can figure out what God's will is—what is good
and pleasing and mature.

—Romans 12:2

Sometimes you may feel like a square peg in a round hole. No matter how much effort you put into getting in line with the thinking of the team at your office or the friends in your circle or the people in your Bible study, you're just not on the same page. Is it you or is it them?

It's probably both. It may be a good thing that you're struggling to fit, because the truth just may be that you DON'T. That's okay. Even if the group you're part of is doing wonderful things for the community or building a new vision for the company or finding a new mission, they may not be a part of your unique calling. You don't fit for a reason. God created a little discomfort in you to get you moving again.

You're God's child and so you always fit with him. You fit into a great design that he constructed, and only you can do the part he made you to do. Go out today and be purposeful about your

The uniqueness of you fits perfectly with a perfect God.

choices. Give God every opportunity to shape you and mold you so you fit according to his will and purpose.

QUIET THE WAVES

Lord, help me see what you see. Help me be what you want me to be and give me the courage to be uniquely transformed by your loving hand. Amen.

Won't You Be My Neighbor?

The commandments . . . are all summed up in one word:
You must love your neighbor as yourself. Love doesn't do anything
wrong to a neighbor; therefore love is what fulfills the Law.

—Romans 13:9-10

If you grew up in a neighborhood, or you watched Mr. Rogers as a kid, you might think that neighbors are those people who live on your block. They're the people who watch out for your house when you're out of town and the ones who stop by with a gift on your birthday. They know you and love you.

But these are not your only neighbors. You have neighbors at work, people who have an office next to yours. Your newspaper carrier and your hairdresser are also your neighbors, and so is the guy three states over who isn't on your Christmas card list.

Today's a good day to expand your definition of a neighbor. Touch the life of someone you meet at the local coffee shop or someone who sits by you on the subway. Take some groceries to a shut-in. Your neighbors are everywhere, and they're only a thought away.

When Jesus summed up the Ten Commandments with just two, he was talking about love. Love your neighbor as yourself and show God you know what it means to be neighborly.

Your neighborhood is bigger than you imagined.

QUIET THE WAVES

Lord, I am a good neighbor sometimes. I try to watch out for those around me, but I confess that I don't often think about the people I pass by on the street. Help me see them too. Help me reach out in love wherever you lead me. Amen.

Just a Little Humble Pie

Humble yourselves before the Lord, and he will lift you up.

—James 4:10

Did you ever have to eat "humble pie"? Pride can be a tricky thing. It can slither into our hearts like a snake on its belly, giving us the illusion that we're okay. Eve may have needed to eat a little humble pie after listening to the snake in the garden. After all, didn't the snake simply appeal to her ego, her pride, when he seduced her into taking a bite of the forbidden fruit?

Chances are good that we've all had a taste of this bitter fruit, and like it or not, it rears its head again before we realize it. We can even be drawn into its clutches very innocently.

Pride tells us that we are entitled to things. We have a right to be first or to sit at the best table. We have a right to be heard or to be given special consideration. So, how do we check in with ourselves to see what our egos really don't want us to see?

We humble ourselves before God. We come prostrate before him and ask him to search us and see what is in us that should be weeded out. We seek his guidance to shape and remold us so that we are more in line with his will and his work.

> *Give God all your heart today, letting go of prideful expectations.*

We have no need to put ourselves on a pedestal. Our Father in heaven will gladly raise us up when we seek him with a humble heart.

QUIET THE WAVES

Lord, I know that I am guilty of letting my ego get in the way of things. Help me lay my ego at your feet and step away from a heart filled with pride. Let me boast only of you. Amen.

Figuring Out the Good Guys

A good tree can't produce bad fruit. And a rotten tree
can't produce good fruit. Every tree that doesn't produce
good fruit is chopped down and thrown into the fire.
Therefore, you will know them by their fruit.

—Matthew 7:18-20

It's not always easy to figure out the good guys from the bad guys. They can dress pretty much the same. They can show up on the church board or the corporate executive roster. They can appear to be giving and charitable and kind. The important thing to discover is whether they bear good fruit. You have to find out just what the results are of the things they do.

We've let the idea of good and evil become washed out in our culture. We live in a virtual reality most of the time, never really focusing on the real truth as God might have us understand it. Discernment, then, is kind of scary. It asks us to pay attention. It reminds us that we can best understand others by looking at what they plant and what they harvest.

Good judgment comes from good motivation. When we are motivated by God's Spirit, seeking to know more of him and how he would have us see the various aspects of life, we can be

*U*nderstand others by paying attention to results (fruit) of their action.

sure that we'll recognize the good guys from the bad guys. Seek the kind of wisdom that helps you recognize the real fruit that someone produces. It's okay to go ahead and shake the tree.

QUIET THE WAVES

Lord, thank you for helping me see people as you reveal them to me. I know I don't always get it right, but I pray that you will help me focus on the things that reveal the truth in any situation. Amen.

Getting the Best Treatment

Therefore, you should treat people in the same way that you want people to treat you; this is the Law and the Prophets.

—Matthew 7:12

You teach people how to treat you! Your behavior causes a similar behavior in people around you. In other words, your presence, your posture, your smile make a big difference in how any encounter you have with someone will go. When you offer your best self, show your best light, it returns to you in like manner . . . usually.

Matthew is reminding us that we need to always be aware of the other guy. We need to take responsibility for the way our relationships turn out because we play a big part in their construction. If we want kindness from someone else, we need to bring kindness to the table. If we want friendship to evolve, we need to offer the steady hand of friendship.

Most of us want to be treated kindly and well. We want others to value our efforts and see us as good. We want to win their respect and create trust. These are the things that make relationships possible and valuable.

The best way to treat any other person in your life is to simply remember the way you like to be treated. Look at the way God is treating you.

Sow kindness in order for you to reap kindness.

QUIET THE WAVES

Lord, I know that I can do more to create stronger and more loving relationships with some of the people in my life. Help me be kind and giving, in the same way that you are to me. Amen.

What Are You Thinking?

From now on, brothers and sisters, if anything is excellent and if anything is admirable, focus your thoughts on these things: all that is true, all that is holy, all that is just, all that is pure, all that is lovely, and all that is worthy of praise.

—Philippians 4:8

Have you ever gotten caught in a gripe session? You know, the kind where everyone is grumbling and complaining about life and it appears that there is absolutely nothing to be glad about? How do you feel after that session is over? Do you feel energized and ready to get back in the game of life, or do you feel like just letting everything go because there's really no point anyway?

What you think about and what you take into your consciousness from others is vital to your well-being. When you're around toxic conversations and toxic people, you suffer the consequences. You feel depleted of hope and energy.

Snap out of it! The writer of Philippians has some good advice. Don't think about every bad possible outcome you can imagine and try to cope with living. Be intentional about what you allow into your heart and mind. After all, you own that space and you need to protect it. Think about good, true, and beautiful things. It will make a big difference in your day.

> *C*enter your thoughts on what is good, true, and beautiful.

QUIET THE WAVES

Lord, help me steer clear of the people who see only the dark side of life. I have you, the Light of the World, in my heart. Amen.

When the Waters Stand Still

*The people marched out from their tents to cross over
the Jordan. . . . But at that moment the water of the Jordan
coming downstream stood still. . . . The water going down
to the desert sea (that is, the Dead Sea) was cut off
completely. The people crossed opposite Jericho.
So the priests carrying the LORD's covenant chest stood
firmly on dry land in the middle of the Jordan.*

—Joshua 3:14-17

The people in biblical times might have gotten accustomed to the idea of miracles, but then again, maybe not. When the Israelites were walking in the desert, it didn't take long for them to forget how God had parted the Red Sea so they could cross on dry ground. They seemed to forget how he walked with them in a cloud and in a pillar of fire. They glossed right over the fact that he fed them with manna and birds. They had the miracles, but it didn't mean they had the faith.

Later on, God made the Jordan River stand still. He not only made it stand still, he folded it up so the priests carrying the covenant chest could get across on dry ground. Rolling down the river on a steamboat is one thing. Rolling up the river so people can cross on dry ground is something else.

Embrace the miracle of all God has done in your life.

God is willing to create miracles if that's what we need. In fact, everything about our existence is a miracle if we understand it that way.

QUIET THE WAVES

Lord, you can stop rivers from flowing and keep the earth on its course! Thank you today for the miracle of my life and all you do to intervene for my good through your grace. Amen.

What's in Your Wallet?

No one can serve two masters. Either you will hate the one and love the other, or you will be loyal to the one and have contempt for the other. You cannot serve God and wealth.

—Matthew 6:24

Credit card companies would have you believe that the kind of credit card you carry makes a difference. Perhaps! It's not always easy to recognize the seductive power of being able to spend money that isn't really yours. If your circumstances ever make it necessary for you to live on those credit cards, you start to discover what kind of hold they actually have over you.

Perhaps you don't think you have money issues because you don't even use credit cards, but look again. It doesn't take much to become slaves to our money. We build a lot of our lives around it . . . saving, spending, planning, and dreaming. It sounds harsh, but the truth is in your wallet. What keeps you moving forward? Is it your prayer life, your commitment to the things God designed for you to accomplish, or something else? What seduces you into believing you can do it all on your own?

There's nothing wrong with your credit card as long as you give credit where it's due. As long as you are diligent enough to recognize whether you own it or it owns you.

> *S*erve him with your whole heart and he'll provide all your needs.

You're the child of a King and everything in this world is open to you from your Father's hand. Go to him for anything you need.

QUIET THE WAVES

Lord, it's so easy to be seduced by the things of this world. Please help me see the truth in all I do. Amen.

What Part of No Don't You Understand?

Let your yes mean yes, and your no mean no.

—Matthew 5:37

Most of us are ambivalent. We often say yes when we mean no or perhaps maybe, and we sometimes say no before we understand what we mean by that as well. We struggle, then, with letting our yes mean yes and our no mean no. One writer said, "Yes and No are the two most important words that you will ever say. These are the two words that determine your destiny in life."

Wow! That puts the full responsibility back on your shoulders, doesn't it? You've probably straddled the fence now and then, hoping that waiting long enough would present yet another option, but eventually the problem came back again. You had to make a choice.

Owning our choices is the rub, then. It's the place where salt sometimes enters the wound, the place where we wonder at our wisdom or our stupidity to have gotten into the circumstance we're in. We can wonder all we want, but the truth is, we chose it.

> *Choosing to say yes or no determines your destiny in life.*

Consider your choices today. It's time for you to believe in your own ability to choose, to know when your yes means yes and your no means no. Hold steady to the God of your heart in the process. He already said yes to you!

QUIET THE WAVES

Lord, thank you for holding on to me when I make choices. Help me see the wisdom of my thinking so that I can really mean it when I declare yes or no in any situation. Amen.

Don't Worry, Be Happy!

Don't be anxious about anything; rather bring up all
of your requests to God in your prayers and petitions,
along with giving thanks.

—Philippians 4:6

Do you remember that song from Bobby McFerrin that said, "Don't worry, be happy"? In his own way, Jesus told you the same thing. He asked if worrying would add a single hour to your life, or if God dressed the lilies and took care of the birds, why you don't believe he'll dress you and take care of you. Worry only makes you tell stories in your head that may never come true. So how do you stop worrying and be happy?

Henry Ford said, "I believe God is managing affairs and that He doesn't need any advice from me. With God in charge, I believe everything will work out for the best in the end. So what is there to worry about?"

Did you notice how his statement starts? He said, "I believe God." If you truly believe God is taking care of you, that he is totally in charge of the little things as surely as he is in charge of the big things, you have every reason to smile. You can be happy because you have put your troubles in the hands of the One who can actually do something about them.

Trust that God has everything in your life under control.

QUIET THE WAVES

Lord, help me place my life in your hands. Thank you for loving me. Amen.

Faith—What's Enough?

Jesus said to him, "'If you can do anything'? All things are possible for the one who has faith." At that the boy's father cried out, "I have faith; help my lack of faith!"

—Mark 9:23-24

Most of us can empathize with the poor father who struggled with his faith in the story Mark has noted here. We want to believe. In our best moments, we do believe. In our worst moments, we question what we believe. We're not always certain we have enough of this thing called faith.

Alas, we can't buy more faith on the open market, but we may be able to buy into the concept, the idea, the fact of faith in such a way that we do indeed receive more of it. Perhaps faith is something like love. The more of it you give away, the more of it you use, the more you have. If so, why don't we look for every opportunity to share our faith, to ground our faith, to substantiate our faith in such a way that lack is never a problem? When someone we love is ill, we call on our faith knowing that with God all things are possible.

Take a moment and measure your faith quotient today. Is it enough to get you through every twist and turn the day may take? If not, start the day with one request, "Lord, help my lack of faith."

*H*ave faith that Christ Jesus will take you through today's challenges.

Quiet the Waves

Lord, help me depend on faith in you in such a way that nothing can really shake it, nothing can take it away from me. Help me know that with faith in you all things are possible. Amen.

The Message of Angels

But then when he brought his firstborn into the world,
he said, All of God's angels must worship him. He talks about
the angels: He's the one who uses the spirits for his messengers
and who uses flames of fire as ministers.

—Hebrews 1:6-7

If angels are messengers and still making visits to the earth today, God is still actively doing all he can to help us get the message. He may use an angel to remind us that he's there, and when he does we can be sure it's serious business.

The angel stories recorded in the Bible include the angel Gabriel's announcement to Mary about the plan of God to redeem the world through his infant Son, the singing angels at the birth of the baby Jesus, and the angels who helped Peter escape prison. From the Old Testament, we're told of the angels who went out to destroy Sodom and Gomorrah and the angels who killed 185,000 of

Sennacherib's army in a single night. It's safe to say that angels have been busy throughout Earth's history, bringing messages to God's people who are willing to hear them.

God sends his angels to us, because we are of even more value to him than the angels. You were redeemed by his Son and that makes you very special indeed.

> *G*od is ready to speak with you in any way he can.

Bless your angels, thank them for watching over you, and listen for their messages in your own life.

QUIET THE WAVES

Lord, bless my life today and guard me through the loving spirits of your divine angels. Grant me wisdom in all I do and peace in my soul. Amen.

Million-Dollar Questions

What are human beings, that you exalt them, that you take note of them, visit them each morning, test them every moment?

—Job 7:17-18

When we're passing through trials and tribulations, or even rejoicing over incredible good fortune, we're tempted to ask God why. Why indeed does he care about us so much?

We must each answer the question for ourselves, but the facts remain clear that we are important to him. He's been taking note of every detail of our lives since the day we came into being. We're his and there's no mistake about that.

What do human beings, then, want from God? Maybe that's another million-dollar question. Maybe we need to stop and ask ourselves what we get that we wouldn't have without him.

Of course, eternal life pops into our minds pretty quickly, but what about all the other things? To name a very few, we have someone to turn to in prayer, someone we can talk to any time at all. We have someone who sees us and validates our existence and helps establish our purpose. In fact, without God, we have nothing at all.

*W*ho am I, Lord, that you even consider me?

Today, whatever you're doing, give thanks to God for greeting you with each morning sunrise and for desiring a relationship in every possible way with you. Give him thanks and praise!

QUIET THE WAVES

Lord, I am in awe of your willingness to create a personal relationship with me. Let me be all that I can be for you today. Amen.

Ready for Another Round?

But we have this treasure in clay pots so that the awesome power belongs to God and doesn't come from us. We are experiencing all kinds of trouble, but we aren't crushed. We are confused, but we aren't depressed. We are harassed, but we aren't abandoned. We are knocked down, but we aren't knocked out.

—2 Corinthians 4:7-9

If you've ever watched a boxing match, you might relate to the idea that the fighters are in it to win it. They come back for another round after the bell rings, after they've had a little water and gotten their eyelids reshaped so they can see again. They keep at it, because they have just one goal: to win!

We may not get into the ring waiting for the final bell, but we are out there every day fighting. We're fighting for better health, or we're fighting to save a marriage, or we're fighting to get our kids on the right track. We're trying to be the last one standing and the first one smiling.

We may get confused or even crushed temporarily as we receive a blow we didn't expect, but the good news is that we may get knocked down, but with God's help we won't get knocked out. He is there, fighting with us, advising us and shaping the way things go. He is there to help us win, to fight the good fight.

Your God has already won, and you're on his team.

Whatever you're facing, whatever is going on in the ring around you, remember that you're not alone. You two have some good sparring to do with your opponents, and it's going to turn out great.

QUIET THE WAVES

Lord, thank you for jumping into the ring with me, helping me stand when I feel faint. I know I can't do it without you. Amen.

Where Are the Wise?

Where are the wise? Where are the legal experts? Where are today's debaters? Hasn't God made the wisdom of the world foolish? In God's wisdom, he determined that the world wouldn't come to know him through its wisdom. Instead, God was pleased to save those who believe through the foolishness of preaching.

—1 Corinthians 1:20-21

What suggests that a high IQ directly leads to wisdom? Where do we find those who are the real sages, the ones worthy of our listening ears? According to Paul, we are wise when we come to know God, and in that wisdom, we understand more of what makes us worthy in his sight. The things that stand out in this world, the beautiful people, the brilliant ones, the wealthy ones, may or may not have wisdom. Those who are not as inclined toward a kind of brilliance that sets them apart in worldly ways may yet be the wiser.

God sets his people apart, and he has placed them in every arena of life. He has equipped his own with a kind of wisdom that will brilliantly lead others to his door. That's wisdom. That's what sets the wise at heart truly apart.

> *I*n your wisdom, you responded to Jesus Christ and his calling.

Be wise and seek him in every way you can today.

QUIET THE WAVES

Lord, I have glimpses of wisdom, moments of brilliance, but I know that I don't stay in those spaces unless you lead me there. Grant me greater wisdom in the things I do that please you. Amen.

Blowing Out the Winds of Anger

Be angry without sinning. Don't let the sun set on your anger.
Don't provide an opportunity for the devil.

—Ephesians 4:26-27

Anger loves to tell its story. In fact, it will tell the story to everyone and anyone who will listen. It feeds on itself. It gets hotter with every retelling, simmering in its righteous gravy, certain of its veracity. Before you know it, you'll be overcome by its masterful skill at taking you in. You may not even remember what brought anger to the table, but you let the fire burn every time you open anger's door.

Sure, you have a right to be angry sometimes. You have every reason to be offended when someone does something deliberately against you. You have reason to be livid at betrayal in any of its ugliness, but your rights only last for one day. At sunset, you need to hand any of those toasty embers over to God. Let him figure out the best plan for bringing out some sense of justice.

Be angry if you must, but at the end of the day, let it go and give it to God. Share your heart and your emotions about the things that make you angry the same way you do about the things that make you happy. God cares what is happening to you all the time. Don't give Satan even five minutes of your life.

> *Don't let anger last beyond the setting of the sun.*

QUIET THE WAVES

Lord, I don't always get my angry feelings under control. Sometimes I nurse them, pamper them, and hope to make my case stronger. Help me let go of anger any time it is near. Amen.

Wise, Smart, . . . or Just Dumb Luck?

*So be careful to live your life wisely, not foolishly. Take
advantage of every opportunity because these are evil times.*

—Ephesians 5:15-16

A hundred times a day, we make choices. Those choices range from
the ones that have little consequence to those that are life changing.
Sometimes we choose wisely, sometimes we don't. Sometimes we
have all our wits about us. We pray about a potential choice, look
at all sides of it, talk to others and get advice, and we're ready to go.
Whatever happens, we're sure we've done all we can.

Sometimes we try something that takes a bit of risk, and we
take all the right steps to see it through only to have it blow up. The
good news is we're taught wisdom by the things that we do wrong
and also by the things we do right. Whatever the outcome of our
decisions, we can always learn from the results, and that is where
wisdom lives.

When we come to God with our choices, asking for his Holy Spirit to help guide us, we can be sure we've done what we can to be wise. God knows we need his help, and as long as we know it too, we'll stay on the right track. He knows we're smart, but he wants us to be wise.

*A*sk the Holy Spirit to guide your decisions throughout the day.

QUIET THE WAVES

Lord, thank you for teaching me to be wise. Help me seek your guidance in the things I do so I can avoid acting in foolish ways. Amen.

Teaching People How to Treat You

Treat people in the same way that you want them to treat you.

—Luke 6:31

You can find a lot of self-help books designed to build relationships, to resolve conflict, and to give you insights and strategies about dealing with difficult people. These books are popular because we all struggle with the way someone else treats us. We are baffled when we give them our best and show them concern and love, and they still find ways to offend and annoy us. We wonder at their audacity to treat us unfairly.

Jesus tried to help us with this understanding when he reminded us that a good step is to consider what we want back in a relationship and then to give that to someone else. Think about the way we want to be treated, and be a great example of what we hope for in return. It sounds simple enough in theory, and yet, in practice we often fall short.

If you want friends, be a friend. If you want kindness from others, be kind. If you want love, be loving. It's a good day to let others see you for who you really are, so they can love you with joy because they really know you well.

*L*et others see you as an example of kindness.

QUIET THE WAVES

Lord, help me be myself and share who I am with others in ways that please you and allow others to treat me as I also treat them. Bless this day. Amen.

Go Ahead, Take a Chance!

Send your bread out on the water because,
in the course of time, you may find it again.

—Ecclesiastes 11:1

It's not easy to figure out when to take a risk or when to start something new. Even making an effort can seem overwhelming, and yet, something nags at you, insisting that it's time, that today is a new day and even if you didn't make it work before, you can now. Think of the Nike slogan that implores you to "just do it!"

Procrastination may make sense in terms of giving your new ideas thoughtful consideration. Weighing the odds is a worthwhile use of your time. Getting uncomfortable, though, is a challenge, but the writer of Ecclesiastes doesn't really care. He says get it done. With a little due diligence, in the course of time, you may reap a reward, and you may win the day.

If you don't cast your bread on the waters, you know that nothing can return to you. If you simply cast the bread and walk away, you won't be expectant. You won't recognize the opportunity or be ready for the win. So go ahead. Take a chance on becoming all that God meant you to become and show him and the rest of

Make an effort to step out in faith and expect a return.

the world what you've got. It will renew your spirit, and you'll be in a refreshing stream of opportunity.

QUIET THE WAVES

Lord, I let things pass me by over and over again. Help me take a chance and step up to the plate to get things done. Amen.

Those Lessons from Kindergarten

All the believers were united and shared everything.
They would sell pieces of property and possessions
and distribute the proceeds to everyone who needed them.

—Acts 2:44-45

Remember when you were learning about sharing and getting along with others? Your teacher made a point of telling you to share your toys, to be nice to the person next to you, and to help someone whenever you could.

The classroom has gotten bigger, but the lessons are still the same. Share with others, be kind, and help when you can. It's pretty simple, and yet the grown-up version of us doesn't always aspire to do those things.

Take a look at any area of your life today where you're still withholding, still stocking all the toys you can even if you never play with them. You may discover that you've been really adept at sharing and that kindness is so natural to you that you could still make the sandbox set proud.

You may find that you crave the simple acts of kindness and love that you once knew more than you ever realized. You may want those days to come back again.

Return to those early lessons of sharing and kindness.

Guess what? Those days have never gone away. Share your heart today.

QUIET THE WAVES

Lord, thank you for all that you've done to give me simple joys and pleasures. Open my mind and heart to new ways to share with others. Amen.

The Big Seven

Then Peter said to Jesus, "Lord, how many times should I
forgive my brother or sister who sins against me? Should I forgive
as many as seven times?" Jesus said, "Not just seven times,
but rather as many as seventy-seven times."

—Matthew 18:21-22

Maybe it will work if we forgive someone seventy-seven times, or seventy times seven times, or a million times. The point is that we need to forgive each other. If someone offends you repeatedly, doesn't it seem reasonable that you could actually stop forgiving them?

It does, until you consider what God does. What if God had a quota of how many times he would forgive you for something you had done or for all the things you do? What if God cut you off and left you with no avenue for forgiveness even for one day?

Consider this. Forgiveness doesn't change the past, but it can surely change the future. If you can think of one person who has offended you seven times, you can choose to keep counting the errors, you can sever the relationship, or you can choose to forgive seven more times and seven more times after that. Forgiveness allows a relationship to keep going toward the future. Nothing else can do that so well.

Open your heart to greater joy and love and forgiveness today.

QUIET THE WAVES

Lord, help me be able to forgive those who offend me. Remind me to let go of old stories and move on. Walk with me today, Lord, and forgive me all that I do to offend you. Amen.

The Biggest Blessing

The LORD bless you and keep you. The LORD make
his face shine on you and be gracious to you. The LORD
lift up his face to you and grant you peace.

—Numbers 6:24-26

Isn't it awesome to think that the Creator of the entire universe keeps you in his heart in such a way that he can shine a light in your direction and bless you abundantly any time at all? You may receive his gracious light and peace whenever he looks your way.

Imagine now the light of the Son, shining on you, lifting you up, giving you a peace that passes all understanding. Imagine receiving the blessing right now, today. Once you have received it, take it into your heart and hold it just for a few moments. Let it radiate through your body and mind. Let God's grace lead you forward.

We're so accustomed to the rat race, so plugged into the busyness of life, that we seldom really give ourselves the chance to stop, listen, and invite the King of the universe to join us, to smile upon us, to help lighten the load we carry all the time.

It's a good day to be refreshed, reenergized by his glorious countenance, and then step into the day with great faith and joy. May the good Lord bless you in a big way, every day and always.

Take a break from busyness and invite God's refreshment.

QUIET THE WAVES

Lord, thank you for the gifts that come with your gracious blessing. Thank you for seeing me right where I stand. Help me walk more closely with you today. Amen.

Keeping Your Word

"Lord, why are you about to reveal yourself to us and not
to the world?" Jesus answered, "Whoever loves me will keep my
word. My Father will love them, and we will come to them
and make our home with them. Whoever doesn't love me doesn't
keep my words. The word that you hear isn't mine.
It is the word of the Father who sent me."

—John 14:22-24

Did you ever make a promise and then have to go back on it for reasons not your own? Did you ever simply choose to not keep a promise? What does it mean then for us to love God so much that we would keep his word?

Part of keeping God's word means that we open our hearts to give him room to come in and share our lives. It means we are aware of him in all we do and that we seek his guidance above all else. He gave us the opportunity to keep his word with the Scriptures.

God made many promises to us, and we can be sure he will keep his word. We need to pay attention when we make promises. We have to be sure that we mean what we say and that we're ready to carry out any agreements we make.

> *K*eep your promises as God keeps all his promises.

Try today to be very aware of any promises you make, and do your best to honor them. Remind yourself that there is no circumstance that will prevent God from keeping his word at the appointed time. It's a two-way proposition.

QUIET THE WAVES

Lord, help me remember all that you have promised me and all that I have promised you and those who are dear to me. Let me always be willing to keep your word. Amen.

Now, Isn't That Tempting?

So those who think they are standing need to watch out or else they may fall. No temptation has seized you that isn't common for people. But God is faithful. He won't allow you to be tempted beyond your abilities. Instead, with the temptation, God will also supply a way out so that you will be able to endure it.

—1 Corinthians 10:12-13

It would be great to believe that we're too smart to get caught up in the things that tempt ordinary people. After all, we're believers and so we know we will make better choices.

Big temptations can strike us when we least expect them. It may come in the form of not being fully transparent with the IRS at tax time, or withholding affection from your spouse so that you can manipulate a situation to get the outcome you want. It's a form of temptation because it's contrary to what helps to create a loving relationship.

We receive help for the dilemma of temptation through our faith. Thomas à Kempis said, "Little by little, with patience and fortitude, and with the help of God, you will sooner overcome temptations than with your own strength and persistence."

God gives you the abilities to resist temptations facing you.

You're not alone today as you face the temptations that may spiral around you. Call on the God of your heart to help you any time you feel tempted.

QUIET THE WAVES

Lord, I don't even know sometimes that I'm vulnerable to temptation, and then suddenly it rears its ugly head. Help me stay faithful and true to you and to myself in you. Amen.

Pass the Salt, Please!

You are the salt of the earth. But if salt loses its saltiness,
how will it become salty again?

—Matthew 5:13

Salt has always been a precious commodity. In ancient times, it was a bit like gold, because it was valuable for so many things. It not only enhanced the flavor of food, it also was necessary for the good health of the body, and it helped preserve meat and other foods from spoiling. In more contemporary times, even into the latter twentieth century, salt was measured and given to royalty when it was not available to anyone else. Kings and queens often had lavish salt dishes to impress their guests.

Even though salt cannot actually lose its flavor, it can be mixed with other things (as dishonest merchants did) and then lose its effectiveness. Perhaps Jesus referred to that idea when he spoke about salt in the passage shown here.

Today, you may be "the salt of the earth" if you're simply a good person, but you're more apt to be the salt for God if you're out to add richness and flavor to someone else's spirit. It's important to watch what you mix with your saltiness, to protect the effect you're able to have on others. If you create opportunities and spread the joy of God's love, you act as the salt.

Be the salt for your heavenly Father today.

QUIET THE WAVES

Lord, help me enrich others, offering a way to taste your goodness any chance I get. Thanks for passing your salt of joy to me. Amen.

Gobbling Up the Word

*Just as the rain and the snow come down from the sky
and don't return there without watering the earth, making it
conceive and yield plants and providing seed to the sower
and food to the eater, so is my word that comes from my mouth;
it does not return to me empty.*

—Isaiah 55:10-11

Splash! Imagine a cascade of raindrops moving down the window. As you look past it out into the backyard, you can see the grass soaking in its goodness. The birds are shaking the rain off their wings, getting some nourishing sips as they go, and the flowers are closed up a bit, letting the water wash over them, preparing to open up and be even more radiant when the sun comes back again.

You may feel too busy some days to go and renew your Spirit with Bible reading. If you do, think of what you're missing in the same way you would miss having dinner or drinking a glass of water when you're thirsty. God knows you're always thirsting for him in one way or another, and so he has provided a way to be close to him.

Like the birds and the flowers dancing amidst the raindrops, growing and flying and trusting their Creator, you are the object of his love. Go ahead, take in the refreshment he offers right now. It'll do you good!

Take nourishment provided by reading God's Word.

QUIET THE WAVES

Lord, thank you for giving me your Word to help renew my trust, my faith, and my sense of all that is possible with you. I praise you and thank you for showering me with continual blessings. Amen.

You Can Be Right . . . Or Righteous!

Don't let something you consider to be good be criticized as wrong. God's kingdom isn't about eating food and drinking but about righteousness, peace, and joy in the Holy Spirit. Whoever serves Christ this way pleases God and gets human approval.

—Romans 14:16-18

Do you ever catch yourself trying a little too hard to be right? You want the other person to acknowledge that your way is the right way. What you believe is what you believe, and it's just that black and white to you. The problem is that we all come from different cultures. Some of us think it's okay to eat squid and snails. Some of us don't. But we just love to debate our "right-ness."

What's right in God's view, though, has little to do with what we eat or drink. God is after our righteousness. He wants our hearts to be right because then our actions follow. Martin Luther said, "Paul teaches us that the righteousness of God revealed in the gospel is passive, given to us in Christ. As this truth dawned, I felt I was born again, and was entering . . . paradise itself. The whole face of scripture changed. Just as much as I had hated the phrase 'the righteousness of God,' I now loved it—it seemed the sweetest and most joyous phrase ever written."

> *Make your heart right so your action may also be right.*

As you seek to know more of God and his ways, give him thanks for his righteousness and his great love that allows you to be right in your own circumstances.

QUIET THE WAVES

Lord, thank you too for showing us what it means to be righteous in you. Amen.

Don't Look Back!

After getting them out, the men said, "Save your lives!
Don't look back! And don't stay in the valley. Escape to the
mountains so that you are not swept away." . . . When Lot's wife
looked back, she turned into a pillar of salt.

—Genesis 19:17, 26

Warning! Danger ahead! Do you ever wish you had some warning signs posted all around you when you're about to do something really stupid? You may have been given ample explanation for why you must follow the rules to the letter, but you're still tempted to bend the rules a little bit.

Unfortunately for Lot's wife, trying to bend the rules was a deal breaker. God no longer protected her, and the harsh destruction of Sodom and Gomorrah fell on her like acid rain. She had been warned not to look back, but she couldn't resist the temptation to turn around and see what was happening. She became a standing pillar of salt.

Lot's wife isn't the only one tempted to look back. We hold on to old hurts, old stories, or people who betrayed us. We keep looking back, revisiting the storms and destruction we've been through, acting like maybe God didn't really forgive us or wondering if the story is still good for a little sympathy.

Look to today and listen for God's voice.

Your marching orders are only about living in the present and moving into the future. Don't look back.

QUIET THE WAVES

Lord, help me keep in the flow of life, doing what you would have me do to live fully and well without looking back. Amen.

What'd You Say?

What fills the heart comes out of the mouth. Good people
bring out good things from their good treasure.
But evil people bring out evil things from their evil treasure.

—Matthew 12:34-35

Pascal remarked that "kind words do not cost much, yet they accomplish much." What does it mean to you when someone says the right thing at the right time? Words of encouragement and support, words of love and caring are all part of what cause us to thrive as human beings. The words that come from the heart of a loving person offer healing.

It's not surprising then that what we speak to each other is so important. What you say can stay in the mind and heart of another person for all the years of their life. If you offer good words, kind thoughts, and loving messages, then you add to the health and positive growth of someone else. If you allow the harsh words, the negative attitudes, and the cruel behaviors to come out, you can crush the spirit and change the way that person embraces life.

What you say matters. If you speak from the heart, let it come from a source of love. If you speak from anger or insecurity or from some other depression of the mind, you may do great harm.

Offer someone healing today with a word of encouragement.

Today, you can choose how you will speak and what kind of message you will deliver. Make it a great day for someone to hear from you.

QUIET THE WAVES

Lord, help me speak kindly to others, to give what I can, and to share my heart in truth and love. Amen.

The Source of All Power

By now I could have used my power to strike you and your
people with a deadly disease so that you would have disappeared
from the earth. But I've left you standing for this reason:
in order to show you my power and in order to make
my name known in the whole world.

—Exodus 9:15-16

Niagara Falls is powerful. It generates enough electricity to light up a good share of North America.

Gravity and electromagnetism are also powerful forces. They not only keep you safely walking around on the ground, but they keep the earth in its orbit around the sun. The forces of nature keep everything balanced. They are powerful things.

Love is powerful. It draws you into its grasp, like a moth to a flame, or metal to a magnet, and you can feel powerless to resist it.

Love is the medicine that heals wounds and broken hearts, the tonic that makes everything in life feel better. Love is a powerful thing.

Many things are powerful, from the physical things that God created to make the planet work well, to the simple things that you can generate, like love and compassion. Many things

Know the power of God, the power of love.

are powerful, but there is only ONE source of real power. God is all there is when it comes to power. He rules. Aren't you glad to be one of his children?

QUIET THE WAVES

Lord, there are so many things that make me feel powerless. Yet, you love me, simple as I am, and give me the power to be your child. Thank you for loving me so much. Amen.

Awash with the Spirit

*Jesus answered, "I assure you, unless someone is born
of water and the Spirit, it's not possible to enter God's kingdom.
Whatever is born of the flesh is flesh, and whatever
is born of the Spirit is spirit."*

—John 3:5-6

In the summertime, a lot of people pay extra attention to watering the lawn and working to keep the garden nourished and growing. Some days, when the sun beats down in an unforgiving way, you, as a gardener, may find yourself wilting, and then you appreciate more fully the gift of water. Nothing quite hits the spot as well as a cold, frosty glass of iced tea or cool lemonade on a summer's day.

Imagine how parched and dry your life would be without the refreshing Spirit of the living God. Imagine getting through the dry spells that happen and not having a resource, a place to go to find shade and peace. Jesus told Nicodemus that a human being needed to be washed in the Spirit in order to come into the kingdom of heaven. The body on its own remains thirsty until it is given the living water of God's grace and love.

When you water your garden or sit on the deck with a thirst-quenching beverage, remind yourself about the gift God has given through his nourishing and refreshing water for your spirit.

His love renews you every day and keeps you refreshed.

QUIET THE WAVES

Lord, I am grateful for your refreshing Spirit and the way it touches the dry parts of my life, renewing my soul and reminding me that I never have to be thirsty again. Help me live in a way today that reflects your great love and mercy. Amen.

When the Well Runs Dry

Everything that has been created by God is good, and nothing that is received with thanksgiving should be rejected. These things are made holy by God's word and prayer.

—1 Timothy 4:4-5

A certain French proverb reminds us that "we never know the worth of water until the well runs dry." Most of us are used to having good drinking water. We're used to turning on the tap and filling up our glass or taking a shower and being totally oblivious to the good water we have or the amount we use. We are blessed with abundance when it comes to water.

These days, though, we often see clips of people around the world where water is not abundant. There are many places where people are grateful to have running water, even if it's brown and muddy or if it needs boiling in order for it to be safe.

Whether we discuss water or clean air or a cozy home and a comfortable bed, the truth is that we have come to expect those things in our lives. We've convinced ourselves that we deserve them and that we've earned them. We almost forget that God provides for our well-being in every way, until the day things change.

> *Thank God for the essentials you enjoy today.*

Today, let's thank him for the fresh water that comes easily into our faucets and be grateful that he provides all that is good for our bodies and our souls.

QUIET THE WAVES

Lord, I guess I do take the drinking water I have for granted. I thank you for taking such good care of me and ask that you would bless families around the world with safe and clean water. Amen.

Being Content

Do not desire and try to take your neighbor's house.
Do not desire and try to take your neighbor's wife,
male or female servant, ox, donkey, or anything else
that belongs to your neighbor.

—Exodus 20:17

Let's get things straight. The people in big houses, medium-sized houses, or tiny houses with tin roofs are not any better or any worse off than you are, unless they don't have Jesus. Everything anyone else has is nothing in comparison to what you have in him. You have every reason to feel like royalty and to make your home a palace, because you're a King's kid.

When you're content with what you have, you're not going to be wishing for what someone else has. Paul said that he had learned to be content in every situation, because he knew what it was like to have a lot, and he knew what it was like to have a little. You know too.

Benjamin Franklin commented that "contentment makes poor men rich; discontentment makes rich men poor."

We're rich in the things that really matter. We're wealthier than anything when it comes to what we inherit from our heavenly Father. We have every reason to stop wishing we were someplace

> *We have every reason to be content as heirs to his kingdom.*

else and start loving that God has put us right where we need to be.

QUIET THE WAVES

Lord, thank you for putting me right where I am. Help me to not envy those people or those things that are so fleeting, but be content with all that you give me right here and now. Amen.

Your Heart and Mind

More than anything you guard, protect your mind,
for life flows from it.

—Proverbs 4:23

God created you with a great sensitivity to life. You have empathy for those who struggle, and you offer encouragement to those in need of hope. You have a good heart.

It's not always easy to protect your heart and mind, though. You can be drawn off in a variety of directions with every news report, every job loss, every relationship that goes down the tubes. It's not easy to protect yourself, so people who seek after God have to stick close to him.

When you have a heart for God and for humankind, you seek to make a difference in the lives of those around you. You seek to become more than you were before, and you even seek to embrace the concept of holiness.

You are his work of art, and you are even more: you are a work of his heart. As you embrace the day, ask God to walk with you and watch over you. Ask him to protect your heart from the cacophony of worldly news and views. Ask him to show you where you can open your heart more fully to receive more of what he has for you. Share your heart with God and those you meet today.

Guard your heart by staying close to Christ Jesus.

QUIET THE WAVES

Lord, thank you for helping me become more of what you created me to be. Help me be willing to share my heart and share your love. Amen.

Giving the Spirit the Brush-Off

Rejoice always. Pray continually. Give thanks in every situation because this is God's will for you in Christ Jesus. Don't suppress the Spirit. Don't brush off Spirit-inspired messages, but examine everything carefully and hang on to what is good.

—1 Thessalonians 5:16-21

Of course, we don't mean to, but sometimes we simply ignore the Holy Spirit, actually giving him the brush-off. We're too busy with the work we have in front of us, too busy with parenting, too busy with figuring out what to do tomorrow, to stop and hear what the Spirit has to say.

If we do get a nudge that awakens our memory enough to hear his voice, we may or may not choose to listen. God gave us ears to hear his divine inspiration, to tune into the frequency of his voice. Of course, really hearing it comes much more easily if we actually tune in with frequency. The more we approach him, the easier it gets.

Today is a new opportunity to tune in to your Creator. Listen for his voice, rejoice in all that he has given you, and pray continually. These are the things that really make a difference.

Stay tuned to God's voice by praying throughout the day.

QUIET THE WAVES

Lord, help me rejoice in whatever situations arise today and seek your voice and see your hand in all I do. Thank you for your Holy Spirit and all he does to help me walk more closely with you. Amen.

Stretchy, Flexible, Open Hearts!

We are partners with Christ, but only if we hold on to the confidence we had in the beginning until the end. When it says, Today, if you hear his voice, don't have stubborn hearts as they did in the rebellion.

—Hebrews 3:14-15

You probably don't think of yourself as stubborn. Oh, you may have a few quirks about how things are done or you may have some definite opinions about issues that are neither black nor white, but still, you're not stubborn.

Martin Luther admitted to his own stubbornness and said stubbornness should have been his middle name. We can probably relate, because we too are pretty inflexible about certain things in our lives. We believe we've already cornered the market and that there's no other valid opinion beyond the one we hold. In fact, we can usually find a good Scripture to support our point and make it seem like a divine revelation.

Even if we could find another Scripture to support the exact opposite view, we would be too stubborn to admit it's there. So, the reminder to us here is to listen today for the authentic voice of

> *L*et go of stubbornness and open your heart to God's leading.

our Savior and be open to wherever he leads us. We have to stretch our minds and hearts to meet him even halfway.

QUIET THE WAVES

Father, help me understand when I'm holding on to something that is not your truth. Help me live with an open and loving heart. Amen.

Running to Win

Don't you know that all the runners in the stadium run,
but only one gets the prize? So run to win. Everyone who
competes practices self-discipline in everything.
The runners do this to get a crown of leaves that shrivel up
and die, but we do it to receive a crown that never dies.
So now this is how I run—not without a clear goal in sight.

—1 Corinthians 9:24-26

We live in a competitive world. We play a board game and our opponents do all they can to beat us. We work in an office, and we do all we can to get ahead of the person in the cubicle next to ours. We sometimes even try to out-give each other so that we can claim to be the most charitable or the most Christian. We run to win!

But if we have the right goal in sight, we aren't in the race to get the prize that needs to be dusted or the one that will be spent in just a few days. We're seeking greater treasures, greater rewards.

We want to run the race with the kind of integrity that makes God proud of us.

We want the prize that only he can offer . . . a place with him in the kingdom of heaven. We're all out to win that one, and the only competitor in the race is the one you see in the mirror every morning. Run to win according to God's will and purpose for you.

> *R*un the race to win the prize God has for you.

QUIET THE WAVES

Lord, I want to give you my best self. I want to please you today in all that I do. Please bless my efforts and help me be a contender for the prize only you offer. Amen.

Forever Ago to Forever from Now

The days of a human life are like grass: they bloom
like a wildflower; but when the wind blows through it,
it's gone; even the ground where it stood doesn't remember it.
But the LORD's faithful love is from forever ago
to forever from now for those who honor him.

—Psalm 103:15-17

Perhaps this proverb from the Sanskrit says it best in regard to how we might live our lives day by day. It says, "Look to this day. . . . In it lie all the realities and verities of existence, the bliss of growth, the splendor of action, the glory of power. For yesterday is but a dream and tomorrow is only a vision. But today, well lived, makes every yesterday a dream of happiness and every tomorrow a vision of hope."

It is always a good exercise for us to look at how we are spending our time. What are we doing to make this world a little better? In what ways will we blossom and grow?

We have real, authentic, and important work to do. We have the power to develop those things and utilize those attributes for good any time we choose to do so.

No matter how we leave our mark here, one thing is certain: God is faithful, and he remembers us from forever ago to forever from now. We are part of his bloodline, family members never to be forgotten.

Live this day in a way that will make Jesus proud.

QUIET THE WAVES

Lord, keep me mindful of all that I can do to live well and to share your Spirit in any way I can. Thank you for knowing me and keeping me safe with your love. Amen.

Waters of Joy

The earth will surely be filled with the knowledge
of the LORD, just as the water covers the sea.

—Isaiah 11:9

Although Isaiah wanted us to realize that God did not hide himself and that he made it easy for us to access him, easy to find him, we might still miss the boat. We could find ourselves marooned on dry land, waiting for the day when he'll rescue us from ourselves, waiting for the Living Water.

It may be of interest to also note that potable water, fresh water that we can drink, covers only about 2.75 percent of the earth. That means we can be aware of the water, but we may not yet be able to drink it, to refresh and renew ourselves through it. Jesus is the fresh water. He is the Living Water that will allow you to never thirst again, to never be dry-docked. He is your fountain of life and will keep you covered in joy.

Today, as you consider the waterways that are near you, imagine the great oceans filled with the knowledge of the Lord, and remind yourself once again how much joy you receive from the fresh water that comes to you every day, through the gift of your faith in Christ.

Jesus, the Fountain of Life, covers you in joy.

QUIET THE WAVES

Lord, I thank you for filling me with fresh water to replenish my spirit and help me through this day. Thank you for your grace and mercy. Amen.

Time to Shine Your Armor

Put on God's armor so that you can make a stand against the tricks of the devil. . . . Therefore, pick up the full armor of God so that you can stand your ground on the evil day and after you have done everything possible to still stand.

—Ephesians 6:11, 13

Have you tried on your armor lately? Does it still fit? Getting a little rusty? These days, you may have to suit up more than you once did, because the world is just a bit this side of chaotic and crazy, and the devil is dancing everywhere you turn.

Some of us wear our armor like we would a tuxedo or a ball gown, because we pull it out for special occasions and moments when we're more sure it will be called for. Others of us give it a passing nod as we pick out our morning jeans and tee-shirts. After all, we're just staying home today and can't really get into any trouble.

The truth is that you need your armor all the time, every day. It's your best defense against the moments when someone suddenly challenges your thinking, questions your faith, or makes you feel uncertain about why you believe the way you do. It's your protection against the self-doubt or mild depression that can hit

Put on God's armor to protect you from today's chaos.

you unexpectedly. It's God's gift to you, and it really looks great on you. Pull it out today, and shine it up a bit. You may be surprised at just how comfortable it feels.

QUIET THE WAVES

Lord, I haven't been aware of putting on my armor much lately, but I realize you gave it to me to help me get through each day. Walk with me today no matter where I go. Amen.

Love Is the Best Ingredient

Better a meal of greens with love than a plump calf with hate.

—Proverbs 15:17

Most of us like to entertain, or at least we like to eat. Good food is conducive to good conversation. Friendships blossom, love grows, people are happy. So why do we need a proverb to remind us about this fact?

If you've ever taken part in a meal where everyone sat stone cold and was silent, where no amount of tasty gourmet delights could change the atmosphere in the room, then you understand the point here. You can eat grilled cheese with someone you love and feel like it was a gourmet treat, or you can eat roast duck with someone you don't care for and hardly be able to swallow the mint sauce.

The lesson here is also a good reminder about the attitude we may have toward life. We might think we'd be happier if we had more money or a bigger house or prettier clothes. We might think love comes with more status in a job or in the community. The truth is that love doesn't care about how much money you make or how often you eat at a fancy restaurant.

Love cares about just one thing . . . your heart. If your heart is right, right with God and full of love, salad greens will be morsels from heaven because all will be right with the world.

Serve others with love for a joy-filled day.

QUIET THE WAVES

Lord, I know that I aspire to having more material things and a better job, but help me be grateful for what I have and for the people who love me. Amen.

What's Stealing Your Heart?

Stop collecting treasures for your own benefit on earth. . . .
Instead, collect treasures for yourselves in heaven, where moth
and rust don't eat them and where thieves don't break in and
steal them. Where your treasure is, there your heart will be also.

—Matthew 6:19-21

It's good to have treasures. Yours have probably changed over the years. You've gone from treasuring your baseball cards or your ballet shoes to treasuring the little things that make your house a home. God delights in giving you the things that make you feel joy in living.

The only issue comes in when the treasures start to consume your time and energy so much that they steal your heart away from God. When you live to add to your collection of beautiful things, instead of living to do the work God brought you here to do, you might find yourself treading on dangerous ground.

A. W. Tozer said, "The man who has God for his treasure has all things in one."

It's okay to love your things. It's better yet to love your Creator, who gave you all that you have and who has even greater treasures in store for you in heaven. Help him to stock those shelves every day you live.

> *L*ove your Creator and your treasure is complete.

QUIET THE WAVES

Lord, thank you for giving me such an abundant life. Thanks for all you do to help me grow in awareness of the treasures that I truly have in you. Amen.

Childlike Wonder

"I assure you that whoever doesn't welcome
God's kingdom like a child will never enter it."
Then he hugged the children and blessed them.

—Mark 10:15-16

One of the things most of us love about little children is their approach to life. They see the best of life and believe that they are totally surrounded by love and that they are always protected.

Perhaps in part, that is the kind of innocent love God wants us to have. It's the simple faith that believes in the goodness and the desire of God to want only our good. It's the kind of love that too many adults have laid to rest with fairy tales.

God loves your work as an adult. He loves your maturity and your willingness to take risks for him. He also loves the child within you, the one who keeps going in spite of fears, that faces challenges knowing that your Dad will bail you out if need be.

As you go about your work today, look for opportunities to rediscover the awe of life, the little things that God gives you to make you smile and bring you joy. God may have answered a prayer before you could even ask, simply out of love and because he's always looking out for you.

> *B*e his child today and show him your smile of love.

QUIET THE WAVES

Lord, I probably do get more serious in my thoughts of you, thinking I have to be a responsible adult about everything, forgetting to admire your handiwork all around me. Remind me today to simply be your child in every good way. Amen.

Everyday Moments of Joy

You will draw water with joy from the springs of salvation.
And you will say on that day: "Thank the LORD;
call on God's name; proclaim God's deeds among the peoples;
declare that God's name is exalted.

—Isaiah 12:3-4

What makes you happy? Sometimes it's the special things, the holidays, the moments that are rare and treasured. Other times, it's simply being able to do the everyday, mundane things with ease. Drawing a glass of water from the well, more than likely your kitchen sink, may not seem like a reason to be happy, unless you have been without water for a few days.

Sometimes we forget how happy we are about the little things that life brings. When we do remember, though, Isaiah offers us a way to let God know how pleased we really are. First of all, he tells us to thank God. Thank God for each and every moment that stirs our hearts with joy. Call him.

God's phone is never in need of charging or too busy. You can call him any time, even when you're not in need. You can call him just to share your love. Now that's a good reason to be happy.

Pause in your day to thank God for all he has done.

Quiet the Waves

Lord, thank you for the things that make my life happy and secure. Thank you for loving me just as I am. Help me give all the credit to you for the things that are so good in my life. Amen.

It's a Great Day to Shine!

From the rising of the sun to where it sets, God, the Lord God,
speaks, calling out to the earth. From Zion, perfect in beauty,
God shines brightly.

—Psalm 50:1-2

Augustine of Hippo said, "Ask the earth and the sea, the plains and the mountains, the sky and the clouds, the stars and the sun, the fish and animals, and all of them will say, 'We are beautiful because God made us.' This beauty is their testimony to God."

What is our testimony to God? Do we see the beauty that he has so graciously bestowed on us in the landscapes that surround us and the skies that cover us? Do we see the beauty in others, within ourselves, and in God himself?

The psalmist reminds us that God is perfect in beauty and shines brightly. Perhaps today we can open our eyes to his gifts of beauty. Let's start by thanking God for doting on us like beloved children, making sure we have an environment where we can thrive, giving us everything we need to be nourished and strong. Thank him also for the beauty found in relationships that bless our homes and hearts.

You are beautiful and made to shine bright with love.

God gave us life for one purpose, so we could share in a glorious relationship with him. Let's show him what we can do. Let's be his testimony!

QUIET THE WAVES

Lord, thank you for loving me so much that you allow me to be a light for you. Shine on me so that I can reflect you in all that I do. Amen.

How Big Is Your Belief?

As Jesus departed, two blind men followed him, crying out,
"Show us mercy, Son of David." When he came
into the house, the blind men approached him.
Jesus said to them, "Do you believe I can do this?"
"Yes, Lord," they replied. Then Jesus touched their eyes and said,
"It will happen for you just as you have believed."

—Matthew 9:27-29

We may tell ourselves that if our prayer isn't answered, it simply wasn't God's will, or perhaps he has a better plan. However, this verse is asking more of us than that.

This Scripture puts the ability to believe in the desired result squarely on the ones who are seeking his help. The blind men may not have been able to see Jesus, but they had a vision for what they wanted. They knew that he was the key to changing their lives.

God is in the prayer-answering business. We know that sometimes he gives us exactly what we want. Other times we wait and wonder what to do next or why we don't have more direction. Sometimes we don't feel there was an answer at all. What part did our belief play in getting the answer?

> *B*elieve that God will give you your heart's desire.

Today, let's believe what we really want is exactly what God wants for us too. Let's imagine that and then go to him believing that he will indeed honor our requests. What an incredible day this could be.

QUIET THE WAVES

Lord, I know I need to work on my belief system. I have to trust that you love me so much that you will heal the blindness in any area of my life. I ask you to heal me today, trusting and believing in your willingness to do so. Amen.

Let Your Conscience Be Your Guide

*Some people have ruined their faith because
they refused to listen to their conscience.*

—1 Timothy 1:19

We live in an era where people often act without any trace of conscience. Moral guidelines are given only a perfunctory look, and virtue is no longer espoused as a thing worthy of our attention.

Whatever happened to having a conscience? Jiminy Cricket taught some of us that it was good to let your conscience be your guide. Add to that the idea that the Holy Spirit taps into our conscious selves and tries to offer clear and clean direction. We're not alone here, but we act as though we are. We act as though the things we do have no consequence and whether we please God or not is simply not on the radar.

First Timothy warns us that we can actually ruin our faith, perhaps even lose our faith, when we aren't willing to listen to God.

The still small voice speaks to us, and it serves us well to listen. Today is a new day, and no matter how closely you were listening yesterday, make it your intention to do so now. See what the Spirit of God wants you to know and feel the direction being offered for your soul. Listen carefully because it will do your heart a lot of good.

> *Every day listen to the voice of the Holy Spirit.*

QUIET THE WAVES

Lord, help me tune into my conscience, trusting and believing that you are working to help me live according to your will and purpose. Amen.

Don't Fear, the Lord Is Near!

Look at the birds in the sky. They don't sow seed or harvest grain or gather crops into barns. Yet your heavenly Father feeds them. Aren't you worth much more than they are? Who among you by worrying can add a single moment to your life?

—Matthew 6:26-37

Do you remember a moment in your childhood, perhaps when there was a big thunder and lightning storm, and your daddy wasn't yet home? You may have cuddled up by your mom, just wishing your dad would return because somehow things would be okay then.

Since then, you've weathered a lot of the storms of life, and you haven't always had someone by your side to hold you and help you through. Yet, we're reminded in this scripture that your Father in heaven watches over you and loves you dearly. Because he's near, we don't have to worry. He'll calm the storms and lead the way. He'll bring us safely back to himself.

So put everything that weighs on your heart into words. Without any concern for how those words get to him, simply tell him your story. Talk to him about your life, what you feel concerned about, what you think is missing. The Lord will hear you because he is near. He's always near.

Draw near to the Lord and he will draw near to you.

QUIET THE WAVES

Lord, thank you for being with me today. I believe that you have my life in your hands and that you know all the things that bring me stress or cause me to worry. I ask you to stand by me again and bring me your gift of peace. Amen.